PLAIN FOLK

The Life Stories of Undistinguished Americans

PLAIN FOLK

Edited and with an Introduction by
DAVID M. KATZMAN
and
WILLIAM M. TUTTLE, JR.

UNIVERSITY OF ILLINOIS PRESS
Urbana   Chicago   London

Illini Books edition, 1983
© 1982 by the Board of Trustees of the University of Illinois
Manufactured in the United States of America
1 2 3 4 C   P 4 3

Library of Congress Cataloging in Publication Data

Main entry under title:

Plain folk.

   Edited essays from the Independent published
between 1902 and 1906.
   Includes bibliographical references.
   1. United States—Social life and customs—1865-
1918—Addresses, essays, lectures. 2. Labor and
laboring classes—United States—History—20th
century—Addresses, essays, lectures. 3. United
States—Biography—Addresses, essays, lectures.
I. Katzman, David M., 1941-   . II. Tuttle, William M.,
1937-   . III. Independent (New York, N.Y.)
E168.P7   973.91'1'0922 [B]   81-3026
ISBN 0-252-00884-7 (cloth)   AACR2
ISBN 0-252-00906-1 (paper)

To the descendants
of
Kentucky villages
and
the East European shtetl

Geneva Duvall Tuttle

Andrea Rachel Katzman

Eric Michael Katzman

Contents

The Question of Race

Introduction

In at least one crucial respect, the United States in recent years has had much in common with the country as it was at the turn of the twentieth century. In both epochs, people struggled to come to terms not only with their rapidly changing social, physical, and economic environment, but also with their sense of identity as individual human beings. Central to this latter tension, especially among the millions of immigrants, was the question of how much one should deny of one's past, one's heritage, in order to succeed in the present and the evolving future. To become "Americanized" meant, among other things, learning the English language, perhaps Anglicizing one's name, and responding not to the sunshine, the rain, and the other rhythms of nature, but to the time clock and factory discipline. At the same time, there was obvious value—psychic, emotional, and otherwise—in the older languages, work habits, and cultural traditions. Must one, people asked, give up these things in order to proclaim oneself an "American"? This was, and still is, a difficult question to answer. But for more and more people, at the turn of the twentieth century and today, the answer has been: Be true to your heritage, honor it, and be proud of it.

This tension between one's heritage, traditions, indeed one's "roots," and the everyday demands of mass industrial society had an impact not only on newly arrived immigrants from Russia, Italy, Poland, and elsewhere, but also on people who had lived in the United States for decades—for example, Native Americans, Afro-Americans, and rural-born Americans who had migrated to and were living and working in cities. Indeed, it was an Afro-American, W. E. B. Du Bois, who best expressed this dilemma. Writing in 1897, Du Bois noted that the Afro-American has a "double-consciousness," a "sense of always looking at one's self through the eyes of others, of measuring one's soul by the tape of a world that looks on in amused contempt and pity."[1] Certainly, Jews and Catholics, Russians, Poles, Italians, and Irish, living under the eyes of scornful and nativist Americans, would have agreed. So, too, would the native-born but rural Americans who had moved to the cities, bringing with them their rural world view, habits, and traditions. Country bumpkins, dirty foreigners, ignorant blacks—so they appeared to many native-born and urbanized Americans, who perceived the newcomers to be dangerous people who inhabited teeming, filthy, dilapidated tenement houses, supported corrupt boss-ridden political machines, and agitated for the formation of radical labor unions and even the overthrow of constitutional government in the United States.

Another pressure on the newcomers and their traditions was the eagerness to "succeed," to make money, to rise into the middle classes. At the same time, there were countervailing pressures. These people had reason to be proud of who they were and of the lands from which they had come; their cultures had also produced art, music, literature, science, and technology. In many parts of the United States, they still were doing so, through the establishment of foreign language publications, churches and schools, and cultural and musical societies. Here was the tension, the tug between the old and the new. "One ever feels his two-ness," Du Bois wrote in words that were applicable to all of these "foreign" groups, "—an American, a Negro; two warring ideals in one dark body, whose dogged strength alone keeps it from being torn asunder. The history of the American Negro [and of other racial, religious, and ethnic groups] is the history of this strife,—this longing to attain self-conscious manhood, to merge his double self into a better and truer self. In this merging he wishes neither of the older selves to be lost. . . . He simply wishes to make it possible for a man to be both a Negro and an American without being cursed and spit upon by his fellows, without losing the opportunity of self-development."[2]

Such was the plight of many millions of "undistinguished Ameri-

1. W. E. B. Du Bois, "Strivings of the Negro People," *Atlantic Monthly,* LXXX (Aug. 1897), 194-98.
2. *Ibid.*

cans" at the turn of the century. Such were the pressures and inner tensions that these people had to combat at that time. It was at just this time that the *Independent*, a reform-minded magazine with a national readership, began to publish a series of "life stories of undistinguished Americans." Between 1902 and 1906, the *Independent*, under the editorship of Hamilton Holt, published seventy-five of these autobiographies, or "lifelets." Holt explained that his purpose was "to typify the life of the average worker in some particular vocation, and to make each story the genuine experience of a real person." In addition, he tried to select "representatives" of a great variety of ethnic groups as well as of "the five great races of mankind, the white, yellow, red, brown and black. ... "[3] This was history "from the bottom up"; these were ordinary people telling their own stories.

Obviously, if each of these memoirists had had to write out his or her own story, the list of authors would not have been representative of the wide diversity of ethnic, racial, and occupational groups in America. The United States in 1900 was a semi-literate country composed of millions of people for whom English was, at best, a second language. But Holt had a solution to this problem. "In procuring these stories," Edwin E. Slosson, one of the *Independent*'s editors, explained, "two methods were used: first and preferably, to have the life written upon his own initiative by the person who lived it; second, in the case of one too ignorant or too impatient to write, to have the story written from interviews, and then read to and approved by the person telling it."[4] The *Independent* and its editors were determined not only that each lifelet would be "a representative, and not

3. Hamilton Holt, ed., *The Life Stories of Undistinguished Americans: As Told by Themselves* (New York, 1906), vii. Our current collection of autobiographies or lifelets differs from the original sixteen gathered together in Henry Holt's 1906 *The Life Stories of Undistinguished Americans*. Holt was most concerned to have each type of "race" represented with little or no concern for the larger themes that their experiences illustrated. In selecting lifelets for this edition, the editors scrutinized all eighty of the original *Independent* articles and selected a small group to reprint, some of which appeared in the original collection. While some racial, ethnic, and nationality balance has been retained, the autobiographies illustrate the themes discussed in the introduction. The selections are reprinted as documents in the original style in which they first appeared in the *Independent*.

4. *Ibid.*, 6-7.

exceptional experience of its class," but also that each memoir would be "truthful, both as to facts and mode of thought. . . . "[5] Even without access to that modern tool of oral historians and interviewers—the tape recorder—Holt and the other editors presented an accurate, insightful, and suggestive portrait of individual American experiences and of the socioeconomic life of the United States at the turn of the twentieth century.

Four years after the inauguration of this series, Holt edited a collection of sixteen of these lifelets, which were published under the title *The Life Stories of Undistinguished Americans: As Told by Themselves*. Again, Holt's purpose was to illuminate the lives not of "great" people, not of national leaders, but "of undistinguisht men and women who will never become leaders in this country, but who have made the nation what it is."[6] In book form they received favorable reviews. One reason for the positive reception was that the lifelets served as a mirror in which Americans could see themselves, their nation, and its prospects for the future. As the sociologist W. I. Thomas wrote, "Perhaps the most striking and instructive feature of the narratives is the disclosure of the conditions which make for content and discontent." Thomas also argued that "these stories of foreigners who have become ardent Americans by leaps and bounds do much to modify our prejudice against indiscriminate foreign immigration."[7] Moreover, with the exception of the stories of the black peon and the farmer's wife, these lifelets validated the American Dream of acquiring money and becoming rich. "To live well you must get money," observed the Lithuanian stockyards worker in his lifelet. These undistinguished Americans were certainly in hot pursuit of the dollar, the vehicle of upward mobility.[8]

5. *Ibid*, 7.
6. *Independent*, LXV (Dec. 10, 1908), 1430. Another of Holt's and the *Independent*'s reforms was simplified spelling; this accounts for the word "undistinguisht." Holt was also engaged in reform movements for the initiative and referendum, feminism, labor unions, and international understanding and peace.
7. *American Journal of Sociology*, XII (Sept. 1906), 274.
8. See Rebecca Harding Davis, "Undistinguished Americans," *Independent*, LX (Apr. 26, 1906), 962-64; *Annals of the American Academy of Political and Social Science*, XXVIII (July 1906), 176.

The significance of the publication of these lifelets was that between the Civil War and World War I the United States was self-consciously a nation of immigrants. From 1880 through 1919, the United States drew twenty-three million immigrants to her shores. Most immigrants entered at Ellis Island, in the shadow of the Statue of Liberty in New York harbor. Emma Lazarus expressed the gravitational pull of the United States when in 1883 she wrote "The New Colossus," contrasting the Statue of Liberty with the Colossus of Rhodes, one of the legendary wonders of the ancient world. The Philadephia poet named the statue "Mother of Exiles," and gave voice to her silent lips:

> Give me your tired, your poor,
> Your huddled masses yearning to breathe free,
> The wretched refuse of your teeming shore.
> Send these, the homeless, tempest-tost to me. . . .

So they came, drawn by the beacons of economic opportunity, religious freedom, and hope. In the cities and on the prairies they sought their fortune. Railroad company advertisements, state emigration agents, and letters from relatives and friends in the United States promised success and prosperity; the riches to be found in America where "streets were paved with gold" became part of European folklore. Other immigrants came to practice their religion in the United States because it had no single established church and was more tolerant of religious diversity.

By the late 1880s the pattern of immigration to the United States was signficantly different from that of the earlier period. Between 1860 and 1890, ten million immigrants arrived in the United States, predominantly from the British Isles, Germany, Scandinavia, Switzerland, and Holland. In the peak year of 1882, eighty-seven percent of the immigrants came from these countries. But the fifteen million immigrants who entered the United States between 1890 and 1914 came largely from Italy, Russia, Austria-Hungary, Greece, Rumania, and Turkey. Referred to as the "new immigrants," people from these countries comprised eighty-one percent of all immigrants in the peak year of 1907.

European conditions influenced the ebb and flow of immigration to the United States. Industrialization in northern Europe opened up economic opportunities at the end of the nineteenth century and slowed emigration abroad. Heavy migration to the United States earlier in the century had reduced pressures from overpopulation and removed some of the stimuli for leaving northern and western Europe. The famine and poor crops in Ireland in the 1840s and in Sweden in the 1860s had not been repeated. At the same time, conditions in eastern and southern Europe had encouraged millions of families and individuals to leave their homes to find new lives across the ocean. Not only had many eastern and southern Europeans faced limited economic opportunities at home, but also population in those parts of Europe was expanding rapidly, and small farmers, craftsmen, and peasants could neither support their families nor provide opportunities for their children. In some cases, landlords promoted emigration by dispossessing their tenants. In addition, some people fled to the United States for safety, as did Jews from czarist Russia after 1881. Government-provoked pogroms in Russia destroyed countless Jewish communities and killed thousands. Similarly European ethnic minorities—Germans in Russia, Greeks in Rumania, Macedonians in the Balkans, and Czechs in the Austro-Hungarian Empire—found their ethnic identity repressed and, without a national state, sought freedom in the United States. Moreover, the development of transoceanic steamers brought the cost of the Atlantic passage within the means of large masses of eastern and southern Europeans for the first time; they booked passage either with tickets bought themselves or with those purchased and sent back by relatives already in the New World.

The earlier immigrants, those from northern Europe, had received a more hospitable reception in the United States than did the new immigrants. The report of the Dillingham Commission, established by Congress in 1907 to investigate the shift in immigration, reflected the changed American attitude toward immigration and the new immigrants. The commission reported that there was a fundamental difference in the character of American immigration before and after the 1880s. In the earlier period, immigration had been largely a movement of families seeking permanent homes in the New World.

Northern Europeans, the report argued, had assimilated quickly into American society. In contrast, the new immigrants from southern and eastern Europe were in large part unskilled laborers who had come as transients. Unlike earlier immigrants, they avoided agriculture and congregated in the industrial cities of the East and Midwest, where they clustered in their own communities apart from other Americans.

In dwelling on the "perils" to American society from the new immigration, the Dillingham Commission was wrong but many of its descriptions of the new immigrants were correct. Many of the new immigrants were transients, in part because steamer passage facilitated easy travel back and forth across the Atlantic. On the other hand, those who, like the Jews, had fled religious persecution usually settled permanently in the United States. Most of the new immigrants did settle in cities rather than in agricultural areas, thus stimulating the emergence of ghettos in which ethnic-based foreign-language societies and institutions flourished. Many of the old immigrants, however, had exhibited similar patterns. British and Irish immigrants to the United States, for instance, were no less transient than the new immigrants: between 1881 and 1889, 370,000 Britons and Irish left the United States to return home. Those emigrating from the British Isles also congregated together, forming ethnic enclaves within American society. For example, ethnically based societies and institutions thrived in predominantly Welsh mining towns and English mill villages throughout the United States. These immigrants, too, founded their own churches, groceries, taverns, sports leagues, and newspapers separate and apart from the rest of American society.

What did change radically was the attitude of many native-born Americans toward immigrants in general, and this change found expression in virulent hostility against the new immigrants. The optimism with which Emma Lazarus had penned "The New Colossus" in 1883 had faded by the turn of the century; pessimism over the ability of the United States to absorb large numbers of immigrants had become dominant. The experiences of Americans in a society undergoing transformation from a traditional, mostly agrarian society to a modern, industrial, and urban America was so searing and uprooting that optimism itself became a major victim.

Earlier in the century, Americans had welcomed immigrants. The potential garden beyond the Mississippi lured people to till the soil and to recover the abundance of natural resources. All who could make the journey would contribute to the nation's productivity; through their labor in the garden, unused land would yield harvests. They would become the independent yeoman farmers of the Jeffersonian tradition and, in the process, help shape the new America, a blending of all the finer characteristics of the Old World shaped by the best of the new one. It was an optimistic vision, at least for whites; blacks, Orientals, and Native Americans were excluded.

In the late nineteenth century this optimism began to erode. Industrialization brought in its wake major depressions in the 1870s, 1880s, and 1890s. Labor conflict and violence dramatically undermined visions of a natural harmony between capital and labor. European political radicalism and utopianism in the forms of socialism, communism, and anarchism brought nascent revolutionary stirrings to American shores. Events highlighted and exacerbated these very real fears: the violence of the Molly Maguires in the Pennsylvania coal fields, the national railroad strike of 1877, the 1886 Haymarket massacre, the 1893 Pullman strike, mining strikes in Colorado, and the assassinations of two presidents—James Garfield and William McKinley—all contrasted sharply with the optimistic vision of the pre–Civil War pastoral republic.

Native-born Americans blamed immigrants for these developments. Some attributed economic depressions to the inability of the new immigrants to adapt to American society. Others complained that the immigrants did not work hard enough or that, by avoiding agriculture, immigrants formed a parasitic group within the economy. Some Americans complained that the new immigrants brought conflicts with them from the Old World to the New; their politics or ethnic nationalism or class identity or religion introduced unnatural conflict in what was a harmonious society. The growing distrust of immigrants culminated during the depression of 1893 to 1897. The American Protective Association, founded as an anti-Catholic organization, blamed nearly all of America's problems on the new immigrants. From the well of Congress in Washington, D.C., to the pulpits of churches in the Midwest, orators expressed their loss of faith in the ability of the United States to absorb immigrants or in the wisdom of even trying to do so. In addition, many people now saw the wealth of the United States as finite. Immigrants not only did not contribute to the growing national wealth or productivity, but also, the anti-immigrant argument went, by increasing the population they had reduced the slices of the finite pie of resources available to everyone. Economic recovery in 1897 and the decline of the American Protective Association did not end the debate over the contribution of immigrants. The Dillingham Commission clearly doubted the ability of American society to absorb the new immigrants, and its findings were supported by contemporary theories of race in anthroplogy, so that by the 1920s free entry into the United States would be virtually ended.

While the native-born debated immigration policy, immigrants built and reshaped much of American society and life. They had helped build the American industrial order and, contrary to popular mythology, many of them had settled the agricultural land which fed the burgeoning cities; and they had helped build the railroads and supplied the labor for mines and factories. They had also transformed American politics, introducing the personalized style of clubhouse and patronage politics, and they had altered the political agenda, becoming a voice in state action. They had created new institutions in American society and, by doing so, had introduced the cultural variety and pluralism which have become hallmarks of the United States.

In reshaping American society, immigrants experienced a process in which they themselves were reshaped as well. In immigrating to the United States, they brought with them life-styles and cultural patterns different from the ones they encountered here; the ideals, habits, and rituals of life in their native hamlets and cities differed from the society they encountered after passing through Ellis Island. Once in the United States, immigrants wrestled with the conflict between adapting to American society while trying to maintain their traditional, European customs. Many wished to become "Americanized," to shed the label of "greenhorn" and mirror their image of the native-born, while many others sought to resist Americanizing, to maintain their native languages and life-styles. Settlement in an immigrant ghetto, for instance, could shelter the immigrant from direct and

pervasive contact with American culture. Assimilation in or resistance to American culture, however, were ideal extremes; in reality,
most immigrants accepted some aspects of American society while
resisting others. But the process created a basic tension which became
characteristic of immigrant life.

Cultural tensions were not limited solely to European immigrants.
The American-born were moving as well, from farm to city, from one
region of the country to another, and from city to city; they, too,
encountered new patterns of life and experienced the tensions of the
adaptive-resistance process. For example, Southern black men and
women, Kentucky hill people, and Vermont farm girls all encountered
new cultural patterns in the cities to which they migrated. Even
Americans who remained in their rural surroundings had to deal with
economic and social change. Industrialization and urbanization so
transformed the United States in the late nineteenth and early
twentieth centuries that all Americans—immigrants and native-born,
movers and stayers alike—had to confront changing life patterns. As
producers and consumers, Americans became interdependent on
each other and on regional or national markets. Subsistence farming,
for example, gave way to the staple agricultural system where farmers
grew crops for market and entered the money economy. Railroads
brought their farm produce to market and returned with manufactured
and consumer goods for farmers to purchase. Simultaneously, the
craftsmen's workshops and the apprentice-journeyman-master
system gave way to structured factories and assigned work tasks.
Consumer items were no longer made to order locally; they carried a
fixed price and were manufactured rather than crafted.

Workers in the United States, whether native or foreign-born, had
been accustomed to traditional work rhythms. People in rural society,
for example, had followed such rhythms of nature as the sun and
rainfall. Before artificial lights, craftsmen spent more time at their
benches during the longer daylight hours of summer than in the shorter
daytime of winter. Agriculture obviously had seasonal cycles as well:
intensive seasonal planting, weeding, and harvesting, sometimes
around the clock, followed by harvest holidays and a slower work
pace until the cycle was repeated the following year. The pattern
differed, however, from village to village, as different nationality and

religious groups pursued their own customs and rhythms.

Industrial society changed the structure of work in the United States. Unlike the craftsmen who had made the whole product, such as a shoe or coat or chair, factory workers gathered in large numbers under one roof, performed according to preset rules, and became minutely specialized in making one item or accomplishing one task. In the factory a worker cut soles or sewed buttons or lathed chair legs or merely assembled the final product. Rather than using their judgment or experience gained from years as apprentices or journeymen, or of fitting the needs of a customer with whom they had dealt personally, they now performed impersonal tasks assigned by managers or engineers. Under the factory system control of the work lay with the foreman, not with the workers themselves.

Industrial society imposed new work habits on all workers. The discipline of the clock replaced seasonal and cultural rhythms, and employees worked a fixed number of hours in summer and winter. Factory workers were cogs in a complex machine which required harmony, unity, and subservience to function. Factory managers were thus intolerant of work patterns that encouraged workers, in performing tasks, to follow traditional cultural and ethnic rhythms rather than the preassigned discipline. Bosses, for example, would not tolerate workers who insisted on celebrating their own national holidays rather than reporting to work. Managers insisted that workers had to be trained to adapt to the factory; they needed new discipline, new habits, new attitudes. Bosses clothed the process in the most patriotic of terms: it was Americanization. Those who failed to adapt not only threatened the new American industrial order, the job of building modern America, but denied themselves the fruits of American capitalism.

For workers the process of change was complex and demanding, although the new discipline offered not only economic benefits but also in some cases physical survival. But there was value in tradition as well. Indeed, many people perceived their very identity and sense of self to be indivisible from ethnic, religious, and cultural traditions. The demands of the factory conflicted with familial and kinship ties, religious imperatives, and social customs and patterns.

Many refused to accept the inevitablity of the changes wrought by factory civilization. The most significant labor organization of the mid-1880s, the Knights of Labor, represented, in part, a rejection of the new industrial order. The Knights pictured an ideal society of small shopkeepers and independent craftsmen living and working within a Christian cooperative commonwealth. Similarly many workers sought to escape the new discipline by becoming their own bosses. Seeking to rise in the social order rather than trying to improve their conditions as workers, they identified with foremen and aspired to join the latter's ranks. Or they started their own businesses, substituting intensive labor for a lack of capital. Although few were successful, the slim prospects of success did not extinguish the flame of hope.

Many of the factory workers engaged in a struggle with managers over control of their work tasks and conditions. On a daily basis they resisted the new discipline and habits, continuing to perform tasks according to traditional patterns and absenting themselves from work on ethnic and religious holidays. Some formed labor unions in a collective attempt to exert control over their working lives. Later workers turned to government and, through hours, wage, and safety legislation, sought to check management's powers. These tensions in the workplace between the pulls of tradition and custom on the one hand, and the demands of the modern, industrial society on the other were experienced nearly everywhere in America in the first decade of the twentieth century.

Yet in the face of tension and insecurity, the lives of these undistinguished Americans had value and substance. If at times they lost faith in others, they seemed to maintain faith in themselves. They struggled with themselves and the larger society, with their tensions and insecurities, to make something of their own lives. Their voices, in the written word, are of people proud and self-aware. Their ability to articulate their own lives sets them apart from others of their generation; yet one can easily imagine hearing similar tales from their coworkers and neighbors if we could go back in time and interview them. Unable to do so we should then listen with greater attention to their stories.

Lawrence, Kansas
January 1, 1981

Men at Work

The Biography of a Bootblack:
Rocco Corresca

"The Biography of a Bootblack" is an odyssey of the new immigration. The tale begins in an Italian orphanage, develops in the Dickensian netherworld of Naples, shifts to Ellis Island and an Italian-American padrone (labor agent), and climaxes with a Horatio Alger rise in New York City.

In the 1880s and 1890s the bulk of European immigration to the United States shifted from northern and western European countries as a source to eastern, central, and southern Europe. The cultural, religious, linguistic, and physiological differences between the old and new waves of immigrants were immediately apparent, and many old-stock as well as pessimistic new-stock Americans feared that this new immigration would lead to the degradation of American society.

The background of Rocco Corresca, the bootblack, exemplified everything that the pessimists found so objectionable in the new immigration. As an orphan without knowledge of his background, as a latter-day Oliver Twist begging for food, as an ignorant, superstitious lad and a thief and gambler, he represented an alien threat to the United States. Moreover, he could easily fall prey to the earlier foreign corrupters of American life—the padrone, the union leader, and the political boss—as well as to the saloon and the tenement.

In the end, however, Corresca furnished little support to those who responded to the new immigration with proposals for limiting the relatively free entry into the United States. Corresca, after all, found redemption and success in the United States. He escaped the claws of Bartolo, the padrone, and began a new life cleaning out a saloon. He learned bootblacking and opened his own business with his friend Francisco as partner. They threw off their old ways—learned English, avoided smells of garlic, onions, and red herrings in their shop, saved money, abandoned their expectations of returning to Italy, and filed for citizenship. Corresca was but nineteen when he wrote his autobiography. He had $700 in the bank and dreamed of rising as a capitalist by opening additional bootblack stands.

Corresca did not pay too dear a price in moving from an Italian culture to an American one. His former life, at the bottom of the class structure, hardly offered him resources which he could draw upon or look back to romantically. For many immigrants the process of adapting to a new society and culture was a painful one because there was much of value and comfort in their old ways which they were nonetheless pressured into discarding. For Rocco Corresca, however, the conflict and tensions appeared manageable; the road he chose to Americanization was clear.

WHEN I WAS a very small boy, I lived in Italy in a large house with many other small boys, who were all dressed alike and were taken care of by some nuns. It was a good place, situated on the side of the mountain, where grapes were growing and melons and oranges and plums.

They taught us our letters and how to pray and say the catechism, and we worked in the fields during the middle of the day. We always had enough to eat and good beds to sleep in at night, and sometimes there were feast days, when we marched about wearing flowers.

Those were good times and they lasted till I was nearly eight years of age. Then an old man came and said he was my grandfather. He showed some papers and cried over me and said that the money had come at last and now he could take me to his beautiful home. He seemed very glad to see me and after they looked at his papers he took me away and we went to the big city—Naples. He kept talking about his beautiful house, but when we got there it was a dark cellar that he lived in and I did not like it at all. Very rich people were on the first floor. They had carriages and servants and music and plenty of good things to eat, but we were down below in the cellar and had nothing. There were four other boys in the cellar and the old man said they were all my brothers. All were larger than I and they beat me at first till one day Francisco said that they should not beat me any more, and then

Paulo, who was the largest of all, fought him till Francisco drew a knife and gave him a cut. Then Paulo, too, got a knife and said that he would kill Francisco, but the old man knocked them both down with a stick and took their knives away and gave them beatings.

Each morning we boys all went out to beg and we begged all day near the churches and at night near the theatres, running to the carriages and opening the doors and then getting in the way of the people so that they had to give us money or walk over us. The old man often watched us and at night he took all the money, except when we could hide something.

We played tricks on the people, for when we saw some coming that we thought were rich I began to cry and covered my face and stood on one foot, and the others gathered around me and said:

"Don't cry! Don't cry!"

Then the ladies would stop and ask: "What is he crying about? What is the matter, little boy?"

Francisco or Paulo would answer: "He is very sad because his mother is dead and they have laid her in the grave."

Then the ladies would give me money and the others would take most of it from me.

The old man told us to follow the Americans and the English people, as they were all rich, and if we annoyed them enough they would give us plenty of money. He taught us that if a young man was walking with a young woman he would always give us silver because he would be ashamed to let the young woman see him give us less. There was also a great church where sick people were cured by the saints, and when they came out they were so glad that they gave us money.

Begging was not bad in the summer time because we went all over the streets and there was plenty to see, and if we got much money we could spend some buying things to eat. The old man knew we did that. He used to feel us and smell us to see if we had eaten anything, and he often beat us for eating when we had not eaten.

Early in the morning we had breakfast of black bread rubbed over with garlic or with a herring to give it a flavor. The old man would eat the garlic or the herring himself, but he would rub our bread with it, which he said was as good. He told us that boys should not be greedy and that it was good to fast and that all the saints had fasted. He had a figure of a saint in one corner of the cellar and prayed night and morning that the saint would help him to get money. He made us pray, too, for he said that it was good luck to be religious.

We used to sleep on the floor, but often we could not sleep much because men came in very late at night and played cards with the old man. He sold them wine from a barrel that stood on one end of the table that was there, and if they drank much he won their money. One night he won so much that he was glad and promised the saint some candles for his altar in the church. But that was to get more money. Two nights after that the same men who had lost the money came back and said that they wanted to play again. They were very friendly and laughing, but they won all the money and the old man said they were cheating. So they beat him and went away. When he got up again he took a stick and knocked down the saint's figure and said that he would give no more candles.

I was with the old man for three years. I don't believe that he was my grandfather, tho he must have known something about me because he had those papers.

It was very hard in the winter time for we had no shoes and we shivered a great deal. The old man said that we were no good, that we were ruining him, that we did not bring in enough money. He told me that I was fat and that people would not give money to fat beggars. He beat me, too, because I didn't like to steal, as I had heard it was wrong.

"Ah!" said he, "that is what they taught you at that place, is it? To disobey your grandfather that fought with Garibaldi! That is a fine religion!"

The others all stole as well as begged, but I didn't like it and Francisco didn't like it either.

Then the old man said to me: "If you don't want to be a thief you can be a cripple. That is an easy life and they make a great deal of money."

I was frightened then, and that night I heard him talking to one of the men that came to see him. He asked how much he would charge to make me a good cripple like those that crawl about the church. They had a dispute, but at last they agreed and the man said that I should be made so that people would shudder and give me plenty of money.

I was much frightened, but I did not make a sound and in the morning I went out to beg with Francisco. I said to him: "I am going to run away. I don't believe 'Tony is my grandfather. I don't believe that he fought for Garibaldi, and I don't want to be a cripple, no matter how much money the people may give."

"Where will you go?" Francisco asked me.

"I don't know," I said; "somewhere."

He thought awhile and then he said: "I will go, too."

So we ran away out of the city and begged from the country people as we went along. We came to a village down by the sea and a long way from Naples and there we found some fishermen and they took us aboard their boat. We were with them five years, and tho it was a very hard life we liked it well because there was always plenty to eat. Fish do not keep long and those that we did not sell we ate.

The chief fisherman, whose name was Ciguciano, had a daughter, Teresa, who was very beautiful, and tho she was two years younger than I, she could cook and keep house quite well. She was a kind, good girl and he was a good man. When we told him about the old man who told us he was our grandfather the fisherman said he was an old rascal who should be in prison for life. Teresa cried much when she heard that he was going to make me a cripple. Ciguciano said that all the old man had taught us was wrong—that it was bad to beg, to steal and to tell lies. He called in the priest and the priest said the same thing and was very angry at the old man in Naples, and he taught us to read and write in the evenings. He also taught us our duties to the church and said that the saints were good and would only help men to do good things, and that it was a wonder that lightning from heaven had not struck the old man dead when he knocked down the saint's figure.

We grew large and strong with the fisherman and he told us that we were getting too big for him, that he could not afford to pay us the money that we were worth. He was a fine, honest man—one in a thousand.

Now and then I had heard things about America—that it was a far off country where everybody was rich and that Italians went there and made plenty of money, so that they could return to Italy and live in pleasure ever after. One day I met a young man who pulled out a handful of gold and told me he had made that in America in a few days.

I said I should like to go there, and he told me that if I went he would

take care of me and see that I was safe. I told Francisco and he wanted
to go, too. So we said good-by to our good friends. Teresa cried and
kissed us both and the priest came and shook our hands and told us to
be good men, and that no matter where we went God and his saints
were always near us and that if we lived well we should all meet again
in heaven. We cried, too, for it was our home, that place. Ciguciano
gave us money and slapped us on the back and said that we should be
great. But he felt bad, too, at seeing us go away after all that time.

The young man took us to a big ship and got us work away down
where the fires are. We had to carry coal to the place where it could be
thrown on the fires. Francisco and I were very sick from the great heat
at first and lay on the coal for a long time, but they threw water on us
and made us get up. We could not stand on our feet well, for
everything was going around and we had no strength. We said that we
wished we had stayed in Italy no matter how much gold there was in
America. We could not eat for three days and could not do much
work. Then we got better and sometimes we went up above and looked
about. There was no land anywhere and we were much surprised.
How could the people tell where to go when there was no land to steer
by?

We were so long on the water that we began to think we should
never get to America or that, perhaps, there was not any such place,
but at last we saw land and came up to New York.

We were glad to get over without giving money, but I have heard
since that we should have been paid for our work among the coal and
that the young man who had sent us got money for it. We were all
landed on an island and the bosses there said that Francisco and I
must go back because we had not enough money, but a man named
Bartolo came up and told them that we were brothers and he was our
uncle and would take care of us. He brought two other men who swore
that they knew us in Italy and that Bartolo was our uncle. I had never
seen any of them before, but even then Bartolo might be my uncle, so I
did not say anything. The bosses of the island let us go out with
Bartolo after he had made the oath.

We came to Brooklyn to a wooden house in Adams Street that was
full of Italians from Naples. Bartolo had a room on the third floor and
there were fifteen men in the room, all boarding with Bartolo. He did

the cooking on a stove in the middle of the room and there were beds all around the sides, one bed above another. It was very hot in the room, but we were soon asleep, for we were very tired.

The next morning, early, Bartolo told us to go out and pick rags and get bottles. He gave us bags and hooks and showed us the ash barrels. On the streets where the fine houses are the people are very careless and put out good things, like mattresses and umbrellas, clothes, hats and boots. We brought all these to Bartolo and he made them new again and sold them on the sidewalk; but mostly we brought rags and bones. The rags we had to wash in the backyard and then we hung them to dry on lines under the ceiling in our room. The bones we kept under the beds till Barolo could find a man to buy them.

Most of the men in our room worked at digging the sewer. Bartolo got them the work and they paid him about one quarter of their wages. Then he charged them for board and he bought the clothes for them, too. So they got little money after all.

Bartolo was always saying that the rent of the room was so high that he could not make anything, but he was really making plenty. He was what they call a padrone and is now a very rich man. The men that were living with him had just come to the country and could not speak English. They had all been sent by the young man we met in Italy. Bartolo told us all that we must work for him and that if we did not the police would come and put us in prison.

He gave us very little money, and our clothes were some of those that were found on the street. Still we had enough to eat and we had meat quite often, which we never had in Italy. Bartolo got it from the butcher—the meat that he could not sell to other people—but it was quite good meat. Bartolo cooked it in the pan while we all sat on our beds in the evening. Then he cut it into small bits and passed the pan around, saying:

"See what I do for you and yet you are not glad. I am too kind a man, that is why I am so poor."

We were with Bartolo nearly a year, but some of our countrymen who had been in the place a long time said that Bartolo had no right to us and we could get work for a dollar and a half a day, which, when you make it *lire* (reckoned in the Italian currency) is very much. So we went away one day to Newark and got work on the street. Bartolo came after us and made a great noise, but the boss said that if he did not go away soon the police would have him. Then he went, saying that there was no justice in this country.

We paid a man five dollars each for getting us the work and we were with that boss for six months. He was Irish, but a good man and he gave us our money every Saturday night. We lived much better than with Bartolo, and when the work was done we each had nearly $200 saved. Plenty of the men spoke English and they taught us, and we taught them to read and write. That was at night, for we had a lamp in our room, and there were only five other men who lived in that room with us.

We got up at half-past five o'clock every morning and made coffee on the stove and had a breakfast of bread and cheese, onions, garlic and red herrings. We went to work at seven o'clock and in the middle of the day we had soup and bread in a place where we got it for two cents a plate. In the evenings we had a good dinner with meat of some kind and potatoes. We got from the butcher the meat that other people would not buy because they said it was old, but they don't know what is good. We paid four or five cents a pound for it and it was the best, tho I have heard of people paying sixteen cents a pound.

When the Newark boss told us that there was no more work Francisco and I talked about what we would do and we went back to Brooklyn to a saloon near Hamilton Ferry, where we got a job cleaning it out and slept in a little room upstairs. There was a bootblack named Michael on the corner and when I had time I helped him and learned the business. Francisco cooked the lunch in the saloon and he, too, worked for the bootblack and we were soon able to make the best polish.

Then we thought we would go into business and we got a basement on Hamilton avenue, near the Ferry, and put four chairs in it. We paid $75 for the chairs and all the other things. We had tables and looking glasses there and curtains. We took the papers that have the pictures in and made the place high toned. Outside we had a big sign that said:

THE BEST SHINE FOR TEN CENTS

Men that did not want to pay ten cents could get a good shine for five cents, but it was not an oil shine. We had two boys helping us and paid each of them fifty cents a day. The rent of the place was $20 a month, so the expenses were very great, but we made money from the beginning. We slept in the basement, but got our meals in the saloon till we could put a stove in our place, and then Francisco cooked for us all. That would not do, tho, because some of our customers said that they did not like to smell garlic and onions and red herrings. I thought that was strange, but we had to do what the customers said. So we got the woman who lived upstairs to give us our meals and paid her $1.50 a week each. She gave the boys soup in the middle of the day—five cents for two plates.

We remembered the priest, the friend of Ciguciano, and what he had said to us about religion, and as soon as we came to the country, we began to go to the Italian church. The priest we found here was a good man, but he asked the people for money for the church. The Italians did not like to give because they said it looked like buying religion. The priest says it is different here from Italy because all the churches there are what they call endowed, while here all they have is what the people give. Of course I and Francisco understand that, but the Italians who cannot read and write shake their heads and say that it is wrong for a priest to want money.

We had said that when we saved $1,000 each we would go back to Italy and buy a farm, but now that the time is coming we are so busy and making so much money that we think we will stay. We have opened another parlor near South Ferry, in New York. We have to pay $30 a month rent, but the business is very good. The boys in the place charge sixty cents a day because there is so much work.

At first we did not know much of this country, but by and by we learned. There are here plenty of Protestants who are heretics, but they have a religion, too. Many of the finest churches are Protestant, but they have no saints and no altars, which seems strange.

These people are without a king such as ours in Italy. It is what they call a Republic, as Garibaldi wanted, and every year in the fall the people vote. They wanted us to vote last fall, but we did not. A man came and said that he would get us made Americans for fifty cents and then we could get two dollars for our votes. I talked to some of our people and they told me that we should have to put a paper in a box telling who we wanted to govern us.

I went with five men to the court and when they asked me how long I had been in the country I told them two years. Afterward my countrymen said I was a fool and would never learn politics. "You should have said you were five years here and then we would swear to it," was what they told me.

There are two kinds of people that vote here, Republicans and Democrats. I went to a Republican meeting and the man said that the Republicans want a Republic and the Democrats are against it. He said that Democrats are for a king whose name is Bryan and who is an Irishman. There are some good Irishmen, but many of them insult Italians. They call us Dagoes. So I will be a Republican.

I like this country now and I don't see why we should have a king. Garibaldi didn't want a king and he was the greatest man that ever lived.

I and Francisco are to be Americans in three years. The court gave us papers and said we must wait and we must be able to read some things and tell who the ruler of the country is.

There are plenty of rich Italians here, men who a few years ago had nothing and now have so much money that they could not count all their dollars in a week. The richest ones go away from the other Italians and live with the Americans.

We have joined a club and have much pleasure in the evenings. The club has rooms down in Sackett Street and we meet many people and are learning new things all the time. We were very ignorant when we came here, but now we have learned much.

On Sundays we get a horse and carriage from the grocer and go down to Coney Island. We go to the theatres often and other evenings we go to the houses of our friends and play cards.

I am nineteen years of age now and have $700 saved. Francisco is twenty-one and has about $900. We shall open some more parlors soon. I know an Italian who was a bootblack ten years ago and now bosses bootblacks all over the city, who has so much money that if it was turned into gold it would weigh more than himself.

Francisco and I have a room to ourselves now and some people call us "swells." Ciguciano said that we should be great men. Francisco bought a gold watch with a gold chain as thick as his thumb. He is a very handsome fellow and I think he likes a young lady that he met at a picnic out at Ridgewood.

I often think of Ciguciano and Teresa. He is a good man, one in a thousand, and she was very beautiful. May be I shall write to them about coming to this country.

Brooklyn, N.Y.

Financial Develop of R.C.

poor struggle → rich business man

↓

cope c̄ aversity of

life   → money to live on → Religion

money #
1.
higheclas.
Club
↑.
luxerious

Experiences of a Street Car Conductor

From Chicago to Pittsburgh to Philadelphia to Brooklyn to New York
City, this streetcar conductor moved in search of permanent work.
He was part of that large majority of Americans—men and women in
motion—who moved incessantly, searching for community, security,
opportunity, or social mobility. As a single man without property, he
was among the group who moved most frequently.

The conductor's outlook reflected the conditions of his own work as
well as larger historical currents at the turn of the century. Unlike
factory workers, he worked alone. His job awareness tended to stress
individualism rather than class or job consciousness. He stressed
individualism to the extreme, and in a nineteenth-century fashion
favored the private over the public sphere, as in preferring private over
municipal ownership of streetcar lines. Although he recognized that
private ownership led to a few men becoming very rich, he thought
that the system was the most efficient one. Moreover, he developed a
disdain for the car lines' customers—men and women hardly different
in station from himself—and when he was fired in Chicago and
Pittsburgh he blamed the public, not his employers. He complained
that his soul was not his own, not because the company owned or
demanded it, but because patrons claimed it.

He lacked any sense of class or craft consciousness. The only
fellow worker specifically mentioned was a member of the family with
which he boarded. It is not surprising that this conductor scabbed,
crossing the picket lines and working while a strike was in progress in
Philadelphia. His explanation that he did not like scabbing but had to
work is difficult to take at face value. He ingratiated himself with
management by scabbing and seized every advantage it could bring
him, and when he was temporarily out of work in Philadelphia, he had
no problem finding work elsewhere, this time in Brooklyn. He was one

Independent, LV (Aug. 13, 1903), 1920-24.

worker who felt he could take care of himself alone, without the aid or assistance of anyone else.

WORKING ON the back platform of a street car is generally the last resort of a man who has lost everything but industry. I do not say this to belittle conductors or motormen. I consider it high praise. What I mean is that I know of no form of labor, however difficult, that is harder than working on a street car. Many men who fail in business, cannot make ends meet in their profession, or lose clerical positions, say "No, thank you," when they are offered positions on the cars. They would sooner beg, steal or live off their friends. You may rest assured that the conductor or motorman, whatever his faults, is not afraid of hard work. It must not be assumed that it is easy to secure employment on the cars. In the last few years there has been a slight increase in the pay, and there are hundreds waiting for men to die or resign. Some of them do one or the other, after a while; and now and then—but rarely tho—some man is discharged. In my time, and since the introduction of the trolley in Chicago, where I first went on the cars, there has been a distinct improvement in the class of men who seek the work. And yet the business is not made up wholly of Chesterfields and college professors. It could not be.

Sarcasm? Not at all. Let me illustrate. When I had been railroading a week I had, one night, a very crowded car. A crowd of men and women blocked up the back platform. I called:

"Move up front; there's plenty of room up front."

But they stood there and never moved an inch. I had actually to push them up front. I had been working over ten hours and was not feeling any too well, and I did not use very choice language. When the crowd thinned out and we were near the depot, a man with a high silk hat and a fur lined overcoat came out and lectured me. He said I was rude and he had a notion to report me. He told me I should treat each passenger as if he were my guest, and as if I were anxious he should go away pleased. I was angry and retorted:

"Do you suppose if I could talk and act like that I would be working for $2.10 a day during a blizzard?"

That was enough. He did not say any more; but he reported me, and I did not have a chance to resign.

I could not secure the transfer to another line. Finally I left Chicago, with permission to use the company as reference.

I went to Pittsburg, where I obtained work easily. It paid 24 cents an hour for a day of ten hours, the best wages paid street car men in the United States. I remained in Pittsburg for a year and liked the place. While I was there the papers had a violent discussion over the question of public ownership of street railways. It never amounted to anything. My own opinion is that municipal ownership would not be a good thing. The service generally becomes run down at the heel; the class of men employed is decidedly inferior, and it costs the public just as much in the end. Private ownership means that a few men get very rich; but the service is put on a business basis, the morale of the force is elevated, and the people come pretty nearly receiving the worth of their money.

I do not want you to suppose that I had a sinecure merely because I was satisfied with my position. I have a philosophical nature, and that has always helped me on my journey through life. My little troubles and grievances would fill a good sized book.

A conductor on a trolley car can scarcely call his soul his own. This may sound strange to the casual observer, who regards the conductor as a petty tyrant, lording it over his poor passengers. As a matter of fact, he is subject to the whims of the most insignificant person who enters his car. Any one can report him for incivility or—worse—lie about him, and he has a black mark put down against his name at the office. Then there is that awful book of rules and regulations. Every man employed by the company has to have one, and every man has to learn the regulations by heart. He soon discovers that there is a fine and a threat of dismissal for nearly everything under the sun—except breathing. He finds minute directions telling how he is to act and talk in every possible emergency.

He has to be most careful in case of accidents, whether they are serious or trivial. If John Smith sprains his foot in alighting from the car, the conductor must interview John Smith, and, if possible examine his ankle; and he must secure the names and addresses of five or six persons who saw John Smith sprain his ankle. Of course that is reasonable enough; but the same thing cannot be said of some of the other rules. For instance, if a reckless driver comes along and runs the pole of his wagon into my car, breaking a window, I am compelled to pay for that window. Then again, if Brown's wagon scratches some of the paint off the side of the car, I am compelled to make that good or lose my position.

A conductor's lot is never entirely a happy one. During the summer he risks his life every time he goes to collect fares along the edge of the foot-board on either side of the car. He is liable to collide with a brick pile or a lime kiln at any time; and, when it occurs, he is either killed or laid up for repairs. In the winter time he is on the back platform, half frozen. It is only fair to say that the inclosures around the platform of the cars of to-day are a great protection during inclement weather. I do not believe the companies deserve any particular credit; it took a special act of legislature to make them do it. Then a man never knows when he is going to get a meal. He jumps up before daylight in the morning, gulps down a hurried breakfast, and hurries to the depot to take out his car. He cannot afford to be a minute late. That would be a mortal sin, not to be forgiven. Patti could disappoint an audience, but a car conductor must never fail to be on time for the public. When the dinner hour arrives a small boy who lives in the neighborhood of the conductor's home, or some member of his family, hails the car and passes up the dinner pail. He cannot eat the dinner until he reaches the depot, and by the time he reaches the depot the food is cold. When he is through for the day he hurries home for supper. He is no sooner through than he has to go to bed so that he will not oversleep himself the next morning. It is not a bed of roses.

Being a single man, I was not affected by the loss of home life. I boarded with a conductor's family, and the sacrifices he had to make were really disheartening. He hardly knew his own children, and certainly did not have a chance to enjoy the society of his wife. She was a tidy good-natured woman, who knew how to cook and take care of a house. Her husband earned, on an average, $48 a month, and $12 was paid out in rent for a comfortable two-story house that had a neat bathroom and some other modern conveniences. He kept $5 a month for his tobacco, shaving and other personal expenses. To my way of thinking it was quite moderate. With the remainder, amounting to

$31, she kept the table, clothed the children and provided for her own wants. The $4 a week board I paid her should be added to the total income. I cannot see, for the life of me, how she ever made any money on me; the table she set was enough to eat up the whole $4. She was a natural manager, and with habits of economy was able to do these wonders. That family lived happily and was able to keep out of debt. I do not pretend to say that the family of every railroad man can live so well on the same amount of money. So much depends on the wife. If a man is fortunate enough to marry an industrious and economical woman, she can make ends meet, no matter how much he makes, providing of course, he works regularly and turns the money over to her at the end of each week.   *irreverence for God*

Just when I thought Pittsburg was going to be my home, I lost my position. One day two drunken men boarded my car. They began to sing and soon became profane and abusive. I went inside and quietly asked them to stop. They did stop for a minute, and then became worse than before. Several of the male passengers began to offer hints for my benefit.

"If the conductor knew his business," one remarked, "he would throw these fellows off the car."

"Yes," said another. "But did you ever meet a conductor that had the courage to do his duty?"

This decided me. I went up to the nearest drunken tough—for that is what the man was, inside the clothes—and said:

"If you don't quit your abusive talk you'll have to get off this car."

"I dare you to put me off," he retorted, with a leer and a fresh flow of profanity.   *sharp shrill cry*

I pulled the bell rope, stopped the car, took my man by the back of the neck, and threw him into the street. The women passengers shrieked; the men, sitting as still as Chinese idols, never offered to help me. Tough Number Two came at me. In self-defense I had to fight. When I got through with him he was a sorry vision. I tore his clothes, blacked one of his eyes and blooded his nose. He hammered me pretty hard, too. They had plenty of money, for they hailed a cab and drove off.

When we reached the depot the superintendent was standing there, evidently waiting for me. By his side was the man I had thrown from the car. He looked at me with one-eyed haughtiness and, turning to the superintendent, pointed his finger, saying: *queer*

"That's the man."

The superintendent regarded me quizzically, saying, in angry tones, but with a half smile, lifting the corners of his mouth:

"You are discharged. Take your badge into the office."

"But," I cried, "can't I tell my side of the story?"

"There's only one side to this story,," he replied, grimly. *harsh.*

"Why?" I asked, with open-mouthed wonder. "Because I licked that dirty blackguard?"

"No," he said, lowering his voice; "because the man you licked is the son of one of our directors."

That night I met a man who had two passes east, and we resolved to try our chances in Philadelphia. We got positions at once, only to find out that a strike was going on. I did not like the idea of working as a "scab," but I could not afford to throw up my place. The strike lasted seven days. For two days I did not do a thing, and the other five days I made one trip a day, surrounded by four big policemen and dodging now and then a rotten potato, decayed eggs and an occasional brick, heaved into the back platform by the sympathetic friends of the strikers. I received $2 a day and the assurance of being retained, no matter how the strike ended. The papers said those seven days were a reign of terror; I could not see it in that light. It took nerve to work—that was all. No one was killed; possibly three or four men received scalp wounds from missiles thrown by boys.

The men went back with the assurance that their condition would be bettered. It was not bettered immediately, but it has been since. The pay and the hours are now better than were asked for when that strike was ordered, six years ago. The pay is 20 cents an hour, for a day of from ten to eleven hours. Incidentally, the municipality has exacted good terms from the corporation. The street car companies were given the right to use the trolley system on condition that they would pave and keep forever in repair the streets on which their cars are run. This, I venture to say, has made Philadelphia the best paved city in the Union. *expose to risk of*

Every conductor there is subject to petty annoyances, both from the passengers and the subordinate officials of the company. A rule prohibits us from entering into disputes with passengers, and yet there are times when the observance of the rule is out of the question. A man comes to you five minutes after he has paid his fare and says the change is 10 or 15 cents short. On two occasions, when I felt morally certain that I was right, I gave up the additional money rather than provoke a quarrel and be reported for incivility. A count of my money on those nights proved that I was in the right.

Perhaps the hardest feature of a conductor's life is the "swing" system. By this arrangement, altho a man may only actually work ten or eleven hours, he really has to be on duty for fourteen or fifteen hours. For instance, I take my car out at six o'clock in the morning. I make two trips, which consume four hours, and then I am relieved for four hours. I return at two o'clock in the afternoon and work until ten o'clock that night. But I receive pay only for the time I am actually on my car. I consider this hard usage, and yet I do not suppose it is possible to avoid it.

At one time drunkenness was not uncommon among the drivers and conductors on the street cars, but the introduction of the trolley has changed their habits for the better. A street railway is run now like any other large and progressive corporation. As a result the character of the men is a grade higher than it used to be. Drunkenness is a fault that is never forgiven in a man. If you lost your place through drunkenness to-day and should apply for it in years hence, you would find that black mark still against you. The habits of the average conductor and motorman are good now, and few are dismissed for drinking.

What is worse than riding in a Philadephia street car, especially during holiday times? The people are crowded in like sardines; they trample on toes, and the jerking and the sudden stopping and starting often throw them into one another's laps. A conductor sees it all more vividly than the passengers, because he is a spectator, while the others are the actors. One thing is certain, and that is Americans have a sense of humor—a saving sense of humor. It enables them to bear with all kinds of discomfort and imposition and still feel reasonably happy. They may make a protest—a good, vigorous, verbal protest—but it usually ends there. An American will laugh at a thing that would cause an Italian or a Spaniard to shed blood. This may be platform philosophy, but it comes from years of observation on the back of a street car.

After being in Philadelphia for a little over a year, I was taken with rheumatism, the Nemesis of railroaders. I was laid up for two months. When I went back the superintendent said, in view of the fact that I worked during the strike, he would take me on again if I would wait for two weeks.

I concluded not to wait, and went to Brooklyn, the heaven of the dishonest railroader, where the conductors steal everything but the tracks. I had never been dishonest, so I did not begin there. I stayed in Brooklyn long enough to see that the companies had a network of protection throughout the country against dishonest and careless railroad men, and Brooklyn seemed to be the mouth of the scoop.

My last move was to New York, on the Broadway surface line. I like New York. It's a pretty good town. I think I'll spend the remainder of my days here.

A conductor sees the worst side of human nature. What is there in the atmosphere of a street car that makes men and women, even on Broadway, act with such vulgarity? Why will men spit on the floor? Why do they send their feet sprawling all over, at the risk of tripping up every newcomer? Why do they spread their newspapers out so as to obstruct the view of their neighbors on each side? Why do they quarrel with the conductor? And why do they remain seated while women are standing? And the women—why are they so cross and irritable? Why to they accept a seat from a gentleman without thanking him for it. And why do they try to palm off nine and ten year old children as being "under four"?

But, in spite of all these things, and a good many more, I like my job and I am willing to keep it. To get 20 cents an hour and have the glorious privilege of living in New York is no small thing to me. My health is rugged. I feel that I could almost digest cobble stones. It may seem queer to some persons, but I am sincere when I say that I would sooner be a street car conductor in New York than a leading citizen in a country town.

New York City

A Swedish Emigrant's Story:
Axel Jarlson

Axel Jarlson was ten years old in 1891 when his oldest brother Gustaf emigrated to the United States. Settling in Minnesota to farm, Gustaf wrote letters to his parents and seven brothers and sisters describing a land of plenty where Swedes like himself could prosper. "All about me," he exulted in his first letter home, "are Swedes, who have taken farms and are getting rich." Soon another brother joined him to help homestead sixty acres of farm- and timberland. Two years later, the brothers sent tickets for two of their sisters, and in 1899 one of these sisters, who had married a prosperous Swedish-American in Minneapolis, provided funds for Axel, then eighteen years old, and his sister to emigrate to Minnesota. Here, then, was a linkage—the letter, money, and tickets that connected the old with the new, the past with the present and the evolving future.

What was there about the United States and particularly Minnesota that proved so attractive to Swedes? George M. Stephenson, a historian of Swedish immigration, has written that "the Swedes became Americanized more quickly and thoroughly than other stocks. They had no qualms of conscience in surrendering their birthright in favor of citizenship in the American Republic." Why? Stephenson asked. "Principally because in America they found conditions which nearly approached their conception of an ideal society."[1] The land was rich and plentiful; the climate in Minnesota approximated that of Sweden; and an immigrant in the land of opportunity could accumulate wealth and property. A man in America could vote, and there were "no aristocrats to push him

Independent, LV (Jan. 8, 1903), 88-93.
1. George M. Stephenson, "The Background of the Beginnings of Swedish Immigration, 1850-1875," *American Historical Review,* XXXI (July 1926), 709.

down. . . ." Finally, there was no state church, and many Swedes ignored the warnings of their Lutheran ministers that all that awaited them in America was misery. "Do not go to America!" one such minister had proclaimed to his parishioners. ". . . Those who emigrate to that unhappy country usually meet a terrible fate. They are seized by violent diseases and die in the most extreme distress." And they die alone. "Nobody helps them; nobody comforts them; nobody takes care of them. They sink in the arms of death and their last moments are embittered by the thought that they wantonly deserted their native land."[2]

But then there were the letters mailed home to Sweden from America; negating the warnings of the church, much of the press, and of many parents and grandparents, these letters overflowed with descriptions of happiness, community and fellowship, and prosperity, and they sometimes contained money as well. In addition, immigrants returning home for visits brought with them the material evidence of their success. Axel commented on one such man who wore gold and jeweled rings and had "a fine watch . . . there seemed to be no end to his money." For younger immigrants, the informality of this new land held an attraction, and Axel boasted that in America "you do not have to be always taking off your hat to people." A final reason, which was not peculiar to Axel or to Swedish immigrants alone, was the desire to escape conscription into the army.

By late 1902, Axel, at the age of twenty-two, had established himself in Minnesota. Like his older brothers and sisters, he also wanted to serve as a link between the old and the new. Axel planned to visit Sweden for the Christmas holidays, and he hoped to encourage his remaining brother and sister there to join him on the return voyage. Perhaps in a year or so, his parents, too, "will come to us in Minnesota . . . and then our whole family will be in America. . . ."

I CAN REMEMBER perfectly well the day when my elder brother, Gustaf, started for America. It was in April, 1891, and there was snow on the ground about our cottage, while the forest that covered the hills nearby was still deep with snow. The roads were very bad, but

2. *Ibid,* 708-13.

my uncle Olaf, who had been to America often on the ships, said that this was the time to start, because work on the farms there would just be beginnng.

We were ten in the family, father and mother and eight children, and we had lived very happily in our cottage until the last year, when father and mother were both sick and we got into debt. Father had a little piece of land—about two acres—which he rented, and besides, he worked in the summer time for a farmer. Two of my sisters and three of my brothers also worked in the fields, but the pay was so very small that it was hard for us to get enough to eat. A good farm hand in our part of Sweden, which is 200 miles north of Stockholm and near the Baltic Sea, can earn about 100 kroner a season, and a kroner is 27 cents. But the winter is six months long, and most of that time the days are dark, except from ten o'clock in the morning to four o'clock in the afternoon. The only way our family could get money during the winter was by making something that could be sold in the market town, ten miles away. So my father and brothers did wood carving and cabinet making, and my mother and sisters knitted stockings, caps and mufflers and made homespun cloth, and also butter and cheese, for we owned two cows.

But the Swedish people who have money hold on to it very tight, and often we took things to market and then had to bring them home again, for no one would buy.

My uncle Olaf used to come to us between voyages, and he was all the time talking about America; what a fine place it was to make money in. He said that he would long ago have settled down on shore there, but that he hoped some day to be captain. In America they gave you good land for nothing, and in two years you could be a rich man; and no one had to go in the army unless he wanted to. That was what my uncle told us.

There was a school house to which I and two of my sisters went all the winter—for education is compulsory in Sweden—and the schoolmaster told us one day about the great things that poor Swedes had done in America. They grew rich and powerful like noblemen and they even held Government offices. It was true, also, that no one had to go in the army unless he wanted to be a soldier. With us all the young men who are strong have to go in the army, because Sweden expects to have to fight Russia some day. The army takes the young men away from their work and makes hard times in the family.

A man who had been living in America once came to visit the little village that was near our cottage. He wore gold rings set with jewels and had a fine watch. He said that food was cheap in America and that a man could earn nearly ten times as much there as in Sweden. He treated all the men to brandvin, or brandy wine, as some call it, and there seemed to be no end to his money.

It was after this that father and mother were both sick during all of one winter, and we had nothing to eat, except blackbread and a sort of potato soup or gruel, with now and then a herring. We had to sell our cows and we missed the milk and cheese.

So at last it was decided that my brother was to go to America, and we spent the last day bidding him good bye, as if we should never see him again. My mother and sisters cried a great deal, and begged him to write; my father told him not to forget us in that far off country, but to do right and all would be well, and my uncle said that he would become a leader of the people.

Next morning before daylight my brother and my uncle went away. They had twenty miles to walk to reach the railroad, which would take them to Gothenburg. My uncle had paid the money for the ticket which was to carry Gustaf to Minnesota. It cost a great deal—about $90, I believe.

In the following August we got our first letter from America. I can remember some parts of it, in which my brother said:

> I have work with a farmer who pays me 64 kroner a month, and my board. I send you 20 kroner, and will try to send that every month. This is a good country. It is like Sweden in some ways. The winter is long, and there are some cold days, but everything grows that we can grow in our country, and there is plenty. All about me are Swedes, who have taken farms and are getting rich. They eat white bread and plenty of meat. The people here do not work such long hours as in Sweden, but they work much harder, and they have a great deal of machinery, so that the crop one farmer gathers will fill two big barns. One farmer, a Swede, made more than 25,000 kroner on his crop last year.

After that we got a letter every month from my brother. He kept doing better and better, and at last he wrote that a farm had been given to him by the Government. It was sixty acres of land, good soil, with plenty of timber on it and a river running alongside. He had two fine horses and a wagon and sleigh, and he was busy clearing the land. He wanted his brother, Eric, to go to him, but we could not spare Eric, and so Knut, the third brother, was sent. He helped Gustaf for two years, and then he took a sixty-acre farm. Both sent money home to us, and soon they sent tickets for Hilda and Christine, two of my sisters.

People said that Hilda was very beautiful. She was eighteen years of age, and had long shining golden hair, red cheeks and blue eyes. She was merry and a fine dancer, far the best among the girls in all the country round, and she could spin and knit grandly.

She and Christine got work in families of Minneapolis, and soon were earning almost as much as my brothers had earned at first, and sending money to us. Hilda married a man who belonged to the Government of Minneapolis before she had lived there six months. He is a Swede, but has been away from home a long time. Hilda now went to live in a fine house, and she said in her letter that the only trouble she had was with shoes. In the country parts of Sweden they wear no shoes in the summer time, but in Minneapolis they wear them all the year round.

Father and mother kept writing to the children in America that now they had made their fortunes they should come home and live, but they put it off. Once Gustaf did return to see us, but he hurried back again, because the people thought so much of him that they had made him sheriff of a county. So it would not do to be long away.

I and my sister Helene came to this country together in 1899, Hilda having sent us the money, 600 kroner. We came over in the steerage from Gothenburg, on the west coast. The voyage wasn't so bad. They give people beds in the steerage now, and all their food, and it is very good food and well cooked. It took us twelve days to cross the sea, but we did not feel it long, as when people got over the sea sickness there was plenty of dancing, for most of those people in the steerage were Swedes and very pleasant and friendly. On fine days we could walk outside on the deck. Two men had concertinas and one had a violin.

When we got to Minneapolis we found Hilda living in a large brick house, and she had two servants and a carriage. She cried with joy when she saw us, and bought us new clothes, because we were in homepsun and no one wears that in Minneapolis. But she laid the homespun away in a chest and said that she would always keep it to remind her.

I stayed with Hilda two weeks, and then went out to my brother Knut's farm, which is fifty miles northwest of Minneapolis. It was in August when I reached him, and I helped with the harvest and the threshing. He had built a log house, with six windows in it. It looked very much like the log house where my parents live in Sweden, only it was not painted red like theirs.

I worked for my brother from August, 1899, to March, 1901, at $16 a month, making $304, of which I spent only $12 in that time, as I had clothes.

One the first day of March I went to a farm that I had bought for $150, paying $50 down. It was a bush farm, ten miles from my brother's place and seven miles from the nearest cross roads store. A man had owned it and cleared two acres, and then fallen sick and the storekeeper got it for a debt and sold it to me. My brother heard of it and advised me to buy.

I went on this land in company with a French Canadian named Joachim. He was part Indian, and yet was laughing all the time, very gay, very full of fun, and yet the best axman I ever saw. He wore the red trimmed white blanket overcoat of the Hudson Bay Company, with white blanket trousers and fancy moccasins, and a red sash around his waist and a capote that went over his head.

We took two toboggans loaded with our goods and provisions, and made the ten-mile journey from my brother's house in three hours. The snow was eighteen inches deep on the level, but there was a good hard crust that bore us perfectly most of the way. The cold was about 10 below zero, but we were steaming when we got to the end of our journey. I wore two pairs of thick woolen stockings, with shoe-packs outside them—the shoe-pack is a moccasin made of red sole leather, its top is of strong blanket; it is very warm and keeps out wet. I wore heavy underclothes, two woolen shirts, two vests, a pilot jacket and an overcoat, a woolen cap and a fur cap. Each of us had about 300 pounds weight on his toboggan.

Before this I had looked over my farm and decided where to build my house, so now I went straight to that place. It was the side of a hill that sloped southward to a creek that emptied into a river a mile away.

We went into a pine grove about half way up the hill and picked out a fallen tree, with a trunk nearly five feet thick, to make one side of our first house. This tree lay from East to West. So we made a platform near the root on the south side by stamping the snow down hard. On top of this platform we laid spruce boughs a foot deep and covered the spruce boughs over with a rubber blanket. We cut poles, about twenty of them, and laid them sloping from the snow up to the top of the tree trunk. Over these we spread canvas, and over that again large pieces of oilcloth. Then we banked up the snow on back and side, built a fire in front in the angle made by the tree root and, as we each had two pairs of blankets, we were ready for anything from a flood to a hurricane. We made the fire place of flat stones that we got near the top of the hill and kindled the fire with loose birch bark. We had a box of matches, and good fuel was all about us. Soon we had a roaring fire going and a big heap of fuel standing by. We slung our pot by means of a chain to a pole that rested one end on the fallen tree trunk and the other on the crotch of a small tree six feet away; we put the pan on top of the fire and used the coffee or tea pot the same way—we made tea and coffee in the same pot. We had brought to camp:

FIRST OUTFIT

	Cost
	Cost
Cornmeal, 25 pounds	$0.47
Flour, 100 pounds	2.00
Lard, 10 pounds	1.00
Butter, 10 pounds	1.80
Codfish, 25 pounds	2.25
Ham, 12 pounds	1.20
Potatoes, 120 pounds	1.40
Rice, 25 pounds	2.15
Coffee, 10 pounds	2.75
Bacon, 30 pounds	1.50
Herrings, 200	1.75
Molasses, 2 gallons	.60
Axes, 3	3.55

Toboggans, 2	3.25
Pair blankets	5.00
Pot, coffee pot, frying pan	1.60
Knives, 2	.75
Salt, pepper, mustard	.15
Tea, 9 pounds	2.70
Matches	.10
Pickax	1.25
Spades, 2	3.00
Hoes, 2	2.00
Sugar, 30 pounds	1.80
Snow shoes, 1 pair	1.75
Gun	9.00
Powder and shot	.65
Total	$55.42

"Jake," as we all called the Frenchman, was a fine cook. He made damper in the pan, and we ate it swimming with butter along with slices of bacon and some roast potatoes and tea. "Jake," like all the lumbermen, made tea very strong. So did I, but I didn't like the same kind of tea. The backwoodsmen have got used to a sort of tea that bites like acid; it is very bad, but they won't take any other. I like a different sort. So as we couldn't have both, we mixed the two together.

The sun went down soon after four o'clock, but the moon rose, the stars were very big and bright and the air quite still and so dry that no one could tell it was cold. "Jake" had brought a fiddle with him and he sat in the doorway of our house and played and sang silly French Canadian songs, and told stories in his own language. I could not understand a word he said, but he didn't care; he was talking to the fire and the woods as much as to me. He got up and acted some of the stories and made me laugh, tho I didn't understand. We went to bed soon after eight o'clock, and slept finely. I never had a better bed than those spruce boughs.

Next morning, after a breakfast of cornmeal mush, herrings, coffee and bacon, we took our axes and went to work, and by working steadily for six hours we chopped an acre of ground and cut four cords of wood, which we stacked up ready for hauling. It was birch, beech, oak, maple, hickory, ironwood and elm, for we left the pine alone and set out to clear the land on the side of the creek first. The small stuff that was not good for cord wood we piled up for our own fire or for fence rails.

We found the fire out when we returned to our camp, but it was easy to light it again, and we had damper and butter, boiled rice and molasses, tea with sugar and slices of ham for supper. A workingman living out of doors in that air can eat as much as three men who live in the city. A light snow fell, but it made no difference, as our fire was protected by the tree root, and we could draw a strip of canvas down over the doorway of our house.

So we lived till near the first of April when the sun began to grow warm and the ice and snow to melt. In that time we chopped about nine acres and made forty-five cords of wood, which we dragged to the bank of the river and left there for the boats to take, the storekeeper giving me credit for it on his books at $1.25 a cord. We also cut two roads through the bush. In order to haul the wood and break the roads I had to buy an ox team and bob sleigh which I got with harness, a ton of hay and four bushels of turnips for $63. I made the oxen a shelter of poles and boughs and birch bark sloping up to the top of an old tree root.

By April 15th the ground which we had chopped over was ready for planting, for all the snow and ice was gone and the sun was warm. I bought a lot of seed of several kinds, and went to work with spade and hoe among the stumps of the clearing, putting in potatoes, corn, wheat, turnips, carrots, and a few onions, melons and pumpkins. We used spade and hoe in planting.

The soil was black loam on top of fine red sand, and the corn seemed to spring up the day after it was planted.

We planted nearly twelve acres of the land in a scattering way, and then set to work to build a log house of pine logs. "Jake" was a master hand at this, and in two weeks we had the house up. It was made of logs about 12 by 8 inches on the sides. It was 18 feet long and 12 feet deep, and had three small windows in the sides and back and a door. The ends of the logs were chopped so that those of the sides fitted into those of the front and back. The only nails were in the door. I had to buy the windows. The only furniture was two trunks, a table, a stool and a bench, all made with the ax. The roof was of birch bark.

About the first of June my sister Helene came with a preserving kettle, a lot of glass jars and a big scheme. We got a cook stove and a barrel of sugar, and put a sign on the river bank announcing that we would pay fifty cents cash for 12 quarts of strawberries, raspberries or blackberries. All through June, July and August Indians kept bringing us the berries, and my sister kept preserving, canning and labeling them. Meanwhile we dug a roothouse into the side of the hill and sided it up and roofed it over with logs, and we built a log stable for cattle. A load of lumber that we got for $2 had some planed boards in it, of which we made doors. The rest we used for roofs, which we finally shingled before winter came on again. The result of my first season's work was as follows:

EXPENSES

(From March 1st to December 31st, 1901)

Farm, paid on account	$50.00
Axes, 4, with handles	5.00
Spades, 2	3.00
Hoes, 2	2.00
Oil lantern	1.25
Lamp with bracket	1.50
Oil, 4 gallons	.40
Cow with calf	25.00
Yoke of oxen, with harness, sleigh, etc.	63.00
Seed	12.50
"Jakes's" wages, 6 months	120.00
Helene's wages, 7 months	112.00
Windows for house	6.50
Lumber	2.00
Kitchen utensils, dishes	5.40
Toboggans, 2	2.75
Blankets, 2 pairs	10.00
Pickax	1.25
Mutton, 35 pounds	2.10
Beef, 86 pounds	6.02
Corned beef, 70 pounds	3.50
Bacon, 82 pounds	4.10
Flour, 3 barrels	10.50
Cornmeal, 80 pounds	2.40
Codfish, 40 pounds	3.60

Sugar, 400 pounds	20.00
Oatmeal, 75 pounds	2.25
Molasses, 9 gallons	2.70
Tobacco, 10 pounds	.90
Candles	.10
Tea, 18 pounds	5.40
Coffee, 10 pounds	2.75
Plough	6.50
Rice, 25 pounds	2.15
Preserve jars, 400	7.50
Stump extracting	17.00
Stove	3.00
Preserve jar labels, 500	2.50
All other expenses	21.00
Total	$549.52

INCOME AND CASH IN HAND
(March 1st to December 31st, 1901)

Cash in hand	$292.00
Wood, 45 cords at $1.25	56.25
Preserves, 400 quarts	66.50
Wheat, 67 bushels	46.50
Corn, 350 bushels	163.30
Carrots, 185 bushels	90.45
Turnips, 80 bushels	32.00
Potatoes, 150 bushels	75.00
Total	$822.00
Total expenses	549.52
Balance on hand	$272.48

That comparison of income and expenses looks more unfavorable than it really was because we had five months' provisions on hand on December 31st. We raised almost all our own provisions after the first three months. In 1902 my income was above $1,200, and my expenses after paying $50 on the farm and $62 for road making and stump extracting and labor, less than $600.

I have no trouble selling my produce, as the storekeeper takes it all and sells it down the river. He also owns a threshing machine and stump extractor.

The Frenchman went away in August, 1901. I don't know where he

to separate the grains or seeds
from by some
mechanical mean

is. I have had other good workmen since but none like him.

I studied English coming out on the vessel, but I was here six months before I could speak it well. I like this country very much, and will become a citizen.

One thing I like about this country is that you do not have to be always taking off your hat to people. In Sweden you take off your hat to everybody you meet, and if you enter a store you take off your hat to the clerk. Another thing that makes me like this country is that I can share in the government. In Sweden my father never had a vote, and my brothers never could have voted because there is a property qualification that keeps out the poor people, and they had no chance to make money. Here any man of good character can have a vote after he has been a short time in the country, and people can elect him to any office. There are no aristocrats to push him down, and say that he is not worthy because his father was poor. Some Swedes have become Governors of States, and many who landed here poor boys are now very rich.

I am going over to Sweden now to keep Christmas there. Six hundred other Swedes will sail on our ship. Many are from Minnesota. They have done their fall planting, and the snow is on the ground up there, and they can easily get away for two months or more. So we are all going to our old home, but will come back again, and may be bring other people with us. Some Swedes go to the old country every Christmas.

We're going in the steerage and pay a low special rate because the ships need passengers at this time of the year. We'll have the steerage all to ourselves, and it ought to be very comfortable and jolly. We will dance and play cards all the way over. *good spirit*

Christmas is Sweden's great day; in fact, it is wrong to speak of it as a day because it keeps up for two weeks. The people have been preparing for it since November last. Near our place there are twelve farm houses and about ten people living in each house. In the last letter that I got from my mother two weeks ago she told me about the preparations for Christmas. I know who the maskers are, who will go around on Christmas Eve knocking at the doors of the houses and giving the presents. That's supposed to be a secret, but mother has found out.

I expect to return to America in February, and will try to bring my elder brother, Eric, and my youngest sister, Minna, with me. Eric has never seen a city, neither has Minna, and they don't think that they would like America much because the ways of the people are so different and they work so much harder while they are working.

My father says that Sweden is the finest country in the world, and he will never leave, but he is only sixty years of age, and so he could move very well. Mother is younger, and they are both strong, so I think they will come to us in Minnesota next year, and then our whole family will be in America, for Uncle Olaf is now in New York in a shipping office.

Gustaf is married and has three children, and Knut is to be married in two months, but either of them would be glad to have the father and mother. I think, tho, that they will come to my house.

I am carrying with me two trunks, and one of them is full of Christmas presents from Knut and Gustaf, Hilda and Christine to father, mother, Eric and Minna. When I return to America my trunk will be filled with presents from those in the old home to those in the new.

Among these presents are books of pictures showing Minneapolis, Duluth and New York, and photographs of our houses. My father and the other old men will not believe that there are any great cities in America. They say that it is a wild country, and that it is quite impossible that New York can be as large as Stockholm. When they hear about the tall buildings they laugh, and say that travelers always tell such wild tales. May be they will believe the photographs.

Brandvin is the great drink of the farmers in Sweden. It is a strong white liquor, mostly alcohol, and men can get drunk for very little money in Sweden. That makes some of the old fellows say that a kroner in Sweden will buy more than $2 in America, but that is not true.

Some of the pictures that I am carrying to Sweden are of women in America. They have a better time than in Sweden. At least, they do not have to do such heavy work, and they dress much more expensively. Minna will be greatly surprised when she sees how Hilda dresses now, and I feel sure that she, too, will want to come here and try her fortune, where there are so many rich husbands to be had.

The Swedes who live in America like the old country girls, because they know how to save money.

New York City

Women at Work

A Collar Starcher's Story

As a young woman, the collar starcher found that she had few job opportunities when she left school at sixteen. In the late 1870s only domestic service with its degrading status and restrictive freedom was widely available to women. Thus she considered herself lucky that shirt and collar factories in Troy, New York, were present and open to local women. When she first began to work, she found collar starching enjoyable work. Writing nearly thirty years later, she remembered that factory work offered companionship with the girls she knew from school, church, dances, and picnics. Although the factory had been hot and stuffy, the relatively slow pace of the work had allowed the women to talk and sing on the job. If her memory seemed affected by nostalgia, it must be measured against her experiences in the factory after the introduction of machinery and outside the factory as a young mother twice widowed. Surely no time must have been as carefree and optimistic as those years soon after entering the factory, when her parents were alive and she looked to the future.

Like many young women, she looked to marriage for fulfillment and release from employment outside the household, but her first husband left her a widow with a two-year-old child. After remarriage to a telegraph operator who died of consumption soon after, she became a widow again, this time with two children, for she had been six months pregnant when her second husband died. After the baby was one month old, she returned to work in the factory.

By trade she considered herself a collar starcher, and she found that work more satisfying than any other job. Before her second marriage she had tried clerking in a grocery store but missed the work and companionship of the collar factory. In the article she expressed pride in her work, another factor that compensated for her powerlessness in the factory and the unemployment she experienced outside of the three-month busy season. The introduction of machines to replace the hand work, however, radically changed her situation and attitudes.

New work rules accompanied the machines. The starting hour was moved back to 7 A.M., and the workers felt pressure to appear half an hour before to prepare their work. Foremen forbade talking and singing on the job, and even during lunch hours the workers had to confine their talk to whispers. The machines also increased the amount of work because some work had to be redone by hand. The machines effectively destroyed the old work unit centering around the sense of companionship which women on the job had felt.

The way in which the machines were introduced also struck hard at the collar starcher's sense of self-worth and independence. When the machines were brought in, the work and wage standards were established under ideal conditions. When the work was shifted from hand to machine throughout the factory, wages were cut and ten women were laid off. The women united to protect themselves and agreed to share the work rather than have their sisters laid off. But the women soon realized that this compromise was a defeat: it merely gave their innocent consent to reducing the wage scale which had lasted for twenty-nine years. That they were powerless in this situation soon became apparent. The introduction of machinery and the reduction in the pay scale were arbitrary decisions of the managers. The only way the women could hope to influence their work lives, if not gain control over them, would be to withdraw their labor and strike. The refusal of the head of the firm to see their committee was the final straw; they recognized their situation and struck. All of the laundry and collar workers in Troy realized the threat to their livelihood and, at the time of the article, the industry in Troy was closed down.

The introduction of machinery generally posed two major threats to workers: loss of earnings and reduction in control. In Troy the women were threatened with both. Rarely in the American experience did workers themselves immediately gain from the introduction of machines; the producers' benefits were harvested by the factory owners.

WHEN I left school at the age of sixteen to go to work there were very few opportunities open to young girls, for the time was nearly thirty years ago. Therefore I considered myself unusually lucky to have been born and brought up in Troy, N.Y., where the shirt and collar factories offered employment to women. I was lucky also in being a large, stout girl, for the work offered me when I applied was that of a collar starcher, and while this does not call for much muscle, it certainly requires endurance and a good constitution. In those days practically all the laundry work was done by hand. There were no ironing machines and very few washing machines. The starching was about all there was for a girl of sixteen. So a starcher I became and a starcher I am to this day, or rather, I was until the strike came in May.

I thoroughly enjoyed my first working years. The factory was not at all a bad place. I worked side by side with my friends, the girls I had gone to school with, met at church and at dances and picnics. The starching rooms were very hot and stuffy generally, like a Turkish bath, and the work was hard on the hands; but I didn't mind these discomforts. Looking back at it now I think we were very well off. There was nothing like the rush and hurry we live in now. We were not driven at such a furious pace, for, of course, there was not nearly the business done then that there is now.

The starching itself was a very different affair. The collars were two-ply, instead of the thick, unwieldy things men wear now, and there was no "lady work," as we say. Just men's collars, straight or folded back at the corners—two or three styles are all I remember. We were not obliged to dip those light collars. We simply rubbed in heavy starch, using our hands and soft cloths. It was hot enough, but not the scalding work it is now.

The working hours were not too long—about eight hours a day. We went to work at nine o'clock, except in the busy season, when we were on hand at eight. The day passed quickly with the talk and sometimes a bit of a song to liven things up. We used to sing part-songs and old-fashioned choruses. Some of the girls had beautiful voices.

We have to be at the tables at seven now and an ambitious worker is usually in the factory half an hour before the whistle blows, to get her table ready. As for talk or singing, the foreman would have a fit if anything like that should happen. In our factory all talking is strictly forbidden. You run the risk of instant dismissal if you even speak to the girl across the table. Even at the noon hour you can only whisper. I've seen girls discharged for talking and I know of a case where a girl lost her job for sneezing. The foreman said she did it on purpose. They are not as hard as this in all the factories. Much depends on the foreman.

My father and mother died before I was twenty. We had our little home and my brother and my three sisters and I lived on there. Three of us girls worked in the factories and one sister stayed at home and kept house for us. Our combined wages made a pretty good income. We lived well, dressed well and were very happy. My brother married and went West to live. The housekeeping sister married next and then my youngest sister found a husband. That broke up the home, for the two that were left couldn't afford to keep it up. We took a couple of rooms and did our little housekeeping early in the morning before we went to work.

At this time there came a break in the monotony of my life. I married a young man I had known for a number of years. He was an iron molder and made good wages. We went to housekeeping and I thought my collar starching days were over forever. But my husband was taken ill, and before I realized that he was seriously sick I was a widow with a two-year-old daughter to support.

I naturally thought of the factory, but a friend who kept a grocery store begged me to come to live with her and help her with the business. I was glad to do it on account of my little girl and I did my best to become a good grocery clerk. I cannot say that I enjoyed it, however. It was slow compared with the sociability of the factory, and besides, when you have learned to do one kind of work well you prefer to stick to your trade. I stayed at the store for eighteen months and at the end of that time I married again, a young telegraph operator I met in the store.

You see I have really done my best to fulfill what the ministers and others often tell us is the true destiny of a woman—to be a wife and mother. But the fates have been against me. My second husband had incipient consumption when I married him, altho neither of us knew it. He died after a short illness and six months later my little boy was born. Before the baby was a month old I was back in the factory, a starcher girl once more. Except for this interval of six years I have earned my living starching collars at four cents the dozen.

I have managed to bring up my two children fairly well. They have gone to school and my daughter has had music and dancing lessons.

She is thirteen now and beginning to think of learning a trade. I shall not allow her to become a starcher. My boy is ten. He is very fond of his books and I shall try to put him through the high school. I don't know exactly how it is to be done, especially if the Employers' Association succeeds in cutting our wages in half.

There are many married women and widows in the factories in Troy. Of the married women, some have been deserted and others have gone to work because their husbands could not seem to make a living. It seems to me that in a community where the women greatly outnumber the men the men get discouraged and deteriorate. Very few of the girls in Troy look forward with enthusiasm to marriage. If they are making fairly good wages they hesitate before giving up their jobs. They have too many object lessons around them of women who have come back to the factories after a few years of married life, all their gayety and high spirits gone and two or three children at home to support. It is a mystery to me how they bring up their children so well. I had friends to help me with mine and I suppose the others have. It means sitting up until all hours sewing, mending and washing little clothes. After all, a working mother is like any other woman; she wants her children to wear pretty dresses and starched white petticoats.

Collar starching cannot be classed with unskilled labor. It requires considerable intelligence and a knack of handling the starch so as to get it smoothly through the goods. A poor starcher can upset a whole laundry, for if the collars come out soft from the ironing machines they have to be washed over again. The collars come to us in bunches of a dozen each. We cut the string, dip the collars in a tub of scalding hot starch, throw them on the table, which is covered with a clean cloth, and with the tips of our fingers rub out all the bubbles and wrinkles and force the starch evenly through the linen. Then with a soft cloth we wipe off the superfluous starch and pile the collars in dozens again. They are hung on long bars, which are thrust into drying ovens, after which they go to the sprinklers and ironers. This is mostly machine work, done by young girls. The finishing is hand work and is done by older women.

The starchers work very quickly, of course. They have to, both for the sake of the collars and for the sake of their wages. It is possible to

starch fifty dozen or more a day, depending on the style of collar. I
have often done so. The straight band collar is easier than the wide
turnover. If the work kept up at such a pace a starcher's wages would
amount to ten or twelve dollars a week, but unfortunately, the busy
season lasts only three months in the year. A good starcher makes as
high as fifteen or sixteen dollars a week during those three months.
The rest of the year she is lucky if she makes seven dollars a week. The
average, I think, is about six. The average wage the year round is
between eight and nine dollars.

In order to make good money during the busy season I get up at half-
past five in the morning, prepare a hasty breakfast, leaving the dishes
for my daughter to wash. By half-past six I am at work. In the middle
of the morning I stop just long enough to take a cup of coffee and a
piece of bread, which stay me until lunch time. Ten minutes' pause for
lunch and I am hard at work again. Sometimes I work as late as eight
o'clock. When I get home my daughter has my dinner ready for me. A
year or two years ago I used to have to get it myself after the work was
over. Then, often there was washing to be done, for I am obliged in my
factory to wear a white gown. Dark calico doesn't present such an
attractive appearance, you know.

Many women have it harder than I. One friend of mine has two
children and a bedridden mother to care for after hours, and just before
the strike her husband was brought home with a broken hip.

I am describing conditions in the nine factories which make up the
Employers' Association. These factories supply nearly ninety per cent
of all the collars and cuffs sold in the United States. There are other
factories in Troy, two of which make the highest grade collars
sold. They have refused to join the Employers' Association. These
factories pay better wages than the others and treat their employees
well. Unfortunately they do not launder their own collars. Most of
their work is done in a large independent laundry in the town. This
laundry pays its starchers five cents a dozen for collars. Everybody
likes to work there, for the girls are treated splendidly. They are
allowed to talk and laugh as much as they please, provided they don't
waste their time. In spite of the high wages and the good treatment of
the girls that laundry makes money. It seems queer, doesn't it, when
we are told that our employer's business would go to smash if we were

allowed to speak to the girls across the table?

I have said that a girl in our factory could make between eight and nine dollars a week the year round. The books will show that this is true, but the fact is you can't find out all there is to factory work by looking at the books. You can't find out, for instance, how much of the employees' wages go back to the firm in the shape of fines. To be docked two dollars a week is the commonest thing in the world at our factory. We expect it, in fact, and are thankful when it amounts to no more.

When I go to work in the morning I am given a slip of paper marked on one side "Received" and on the other "Returned." I mark on the one side the number of collars I receive. When the collars are starched I turn them over to boys from sixteen to twenty and they are sent to the drying rods. These boys mark on the other side of the slip the number of collars returned. If a boy makes a miscount or if for any reason at all the numbers do not tally on both sides of the slip, the starcher is docked. The amount docked from her wages is purely arbitrary. If she is short a dozen of work she is charged from fifty cents to a dollar. If the return side contains a dozen more collars than the starcher appears to have received the starcher is docked ten cents and is not paid for the work she is credited with doing. The great majority of the girls are docked every week in this matter of the received and returned slip. The boys are never docked, it being assumed, apparently, that they never make mistakes. But we no longer even wonder why these unjust distinctions are made.

If a starcher drops one collar on the floor she is docked five dozen collars. In other words for every collar dropped on the floor the girl must starch five dozen collars for nothing. The starcher is even held responsible after the collars leave her hands. If the bars on which the collars are dried happen to be dirty the starcher is fined, although the bars are supposed to be cleaned by other workers. If a collar drops from the cleaning bars and is found on the floor, the four girls whose work is nearest are fined. Since it is not possible accurately to locate the careless one the four are punished in order to fine the right one.

These are not all the excuses for docking, but they are the most flagrant and unjust ones. It has been said on good authority that our firm alone has recovered from its employees, in fines, $159,900, during the past ten years. I am not an expert at figures, but I should think that the amount was fully as large as that.

The starchers are no worse off in the matter of fines and hard regulations than the stitchers and banders and other women operatives. In some departments the pay is so low and the fines so excessive that the operatives hardly make a living wage. Yet, for some reason, the starchers alone have been organized. Our union has not been a very strong one and in the two recorded strikes in the last twenty years it suffered from the weakness and dishonesty of its leaders. Our position seemed pretty hopeless last August, just a year ago, when our present troubles began.

At that time several firms in the Association put in starching machines. We had no objection to machines, nor have we now, provided the machines do the work. We would welcome any device which made our task easier or enabled us to turn out more work. I want to make that point clear at the outset.

The machines were brought in but the table starchers were not put to work on them at once. Young girls were brought in from the outside and were set to work in a room by themselves. These girls until just before the strike were not subjected to the same conditions that the table starchers were under. They were given only the easiest work; they were allowed helpers, so that they never had to leave their tables. They were not docked for any cause. In this way they were able to make very fair wages, the payroll, in fact, showing that they received about the same as the table starchers who were receiving larger pay per dozen collars. Then the table starchers were informed that hereafter all starching would be done by machinery and that wages would be cut to two cents a dozen. At the same time they began to lay off ten girls a week.

The great majority of the girls were entirely ignorant of labor union methods. Most of us had never even read any labor literature. But every one of us realized that the time had come when we must organize. The first thing the union did was to agree, instead of having these girls laid off, to share our work with them. We were anxious to retain the girls for more reasons than one. For instance, we were puzzled to understand why they were laid off. We knew that there was no shortage of work, for the firms were actually sending work out to other shops.

We next agreed to try the machines, and we maintain that we did give them a fair trial. They were put in some time in August, and the strike did not come until the 4th of May following. We experimented with them long enough to convince all the starchers including the new ones who had never starched after the tables, that the machines did not and could not starch the collars. The starchers were supposed to only have to rub the work over lightly after it left the machines, but the fact is they had to do as much to the collars after they came out of the machine as they did to the hand starched work. The machine work *unjustic* resulted in stiff welts in the loose linings of the collars, and these welts we had to beat and soak out, and often restarch the whole collar, making the process longer and harder than it had ever been, with a cut of fifty per cent in our wages.

Why should the firms have put in such machines? We asked ourselves the question, and at first it seemed like another of the experiments they try from time to time, experiments which the workers are made to pay for. One such experiment was the use of a certain kind of starch, presumably a cheaper quality than had been used, for the end and aim of all manufacturers is, of course, to lower the cost of production. I shall never forget that starch. It was a German importation. We tried very hard to use it, knowing, of course, that we would be docked if the work was unsatisfactory. It was impossible for us to get it into the linen, and our work all came out soft. We were docked, tried the starch again and were again docked. Then we struck, but our union was too weak to hold out. We went back, tried the starch three days more with the same result and finally convinced the firm that the starch was no good. We paid for that experiment with something like a week's wages.

Knowing the uselessness of combating an experiment we kept on at the machines for a little while after we saw that they could not do the work. The factory was all upside down. One day one thing would be said and the next day another. Three cents a dozen for hand work began to be talked about, and then, all of a sudden, the light broke upon us. The whole thing was clear. The machines were merely a subterfuge to reduce wages. It is not easy to reduce a wage scale which has obtained for twenty-nine years. Awkward explanations have to be made and there is always trouble. The longest way around is the shortest way home in such matters. To put the burden of the reduction on the worker is a clever trick. To bring the thing around in the shape of a compromise is to save a great deal of trouble.

This sort of thing could not go on indefinitely and finally the end came. The table starchers and the machine starchers held a meeting and discussed the situation. We agreed that we could not stand a reduction of fifty per cent. We felt that we should have to grant something to save ourselves, so we agreed to accept a reduction of twenty-five per cent by working after the machines, with bunchers and hangers up, but we were firm in our determination to stand by our old wages for table work. Meanwhile small groups of girls were being discharged and laid off.

We appointed a committee to call on the head of the firm. He refused to let the committee into his office. Twice was the committee refused an interview. Then we struck. The girls remained in the workrooms until one of the firm came in. He said that he had business at the armory and could not talk to them. The leader asked when he would be willing to discuss matters. He said: "You must first go back to work, and I will consider about giving you a hearing at some future date."

The girls refused to go back to work until the matter of discharging and the matter of wages were discussed, and that night they were all discharged.

Several attempts were made to patch up the trouble. The Commissioner of Labor tried to intervene and the State Board of Mediation, I think it is called, did what it could. The Chamber of Commerce also tried. Arbitration was all the girls asked for, but they insisted that the arbitration come before they went back to work. President Shea of the Federaton of Labor and George Waldron, a delegate of the Federation, were chosen to confer with our firm. The firm referred them to the Manufacturers' Association. The Association refused to meet the men but agreed to meet a committee of the starchers. On May 11 the starchers met the Association, and two days later they met them again. Nothing came of either meeting, and a few days later all the girls walked out, not only from our factory, but from the nine in the Association. The machines had not been installed in all the factories, nor had the wages been reduced in all the factories, although we knew that they would be, since the Association exists to kill competition between the factories. The immediate cause of the sympathetic strike was the action of the other factories in taking the laundry work of the factory where the strike occurred. We have been much blamed for this sympathetic strike. As for me, I cannot see the difference between our sympathetic strike and the sympathetic action of the factories in the Association.

We have been out ever since. At first there were small riots. We picketed the factories and tried by all peaceable means to prevent the non-union girls hired to take our places from entering. Some of them turned back ashamed, but others persisted in going in. These girls had their hair pulled and their faces slapped. I am not concealing that. The non-union girls were certainly terrorized. A few of them were handled pretty roughly. We have been denounced for this. Well, there may be better methods of preventing thoughtless and heartless girls from injuring their class, and thereby injuring themselves. There may be, I say, better methods. I wish I knew what they were. Many of these girls were not in the permanent working class. They became strike breakers from ignorance and want of reflection, most of them. Others probably belonged to the class that out of pure snobbery opposes organization. They will not join a union because they do not wish to officially ally themselves with the working classes. There are plenty of women like that. As I said, I wish I knew some way of teachng them their lesson without slapping their faces.

We have allied ourselves with the national body of the Laundry Workers' Union and receive strike benefits from them. Some of the girls, whose sisters are working, voluntarily do without the benefit money; so there is enough to support the others. Some have left Troy and have found work in other towns. The rest of us are still doing picket duty and are holding the union together in all ways we know of. We have every confidence in our leaders.

The sympathy we have met with in the town has been very encouraging. One merchant gave us $500 cash and another gives us $25 a week. Of course most of the merchants are afraid to offend the manufacturers, whose patronage is worth far more than that of the workers. The churches generally are thoroughly down on the strikers and our own ministers tell us that we ought to submit ourselves to the terms our kind employers are good enough to offer us. The head of my firm is one of the most generous contributors to the Y. M. C. A. and has helped build and renovate two churches. He is called an active Christian and is very much looked up to by the best people in Troy. Others in the Employers' Association are splendid churchmen. The Sunday schools and the church societies have a great hold on many of the stitchers and banders. For this reason large numbers of them hold out against a sympathetic strike of the operatives. They tell us privately that they hope we will win and if we do they will probably form unions of their own. That is always the way and we do not complain.

Meanwhile there is one comforting feature: the Employers' Association, in order to save money, is spending it. They have to send all their laundry work out of town to get it done. Some of it goes as far away as Chicago. Their express bills must be something awful.

There is one more little bit of comfort. You ought to see how fat and rosy the girls are getting in the open air. Girls who didn't look like anything are as pretty as pinks since they began to do picket duty.

Troy, N. Y.

The Story of a Sweatshop Girl:
Sadie Frowne

Like the bootblack Rocco Corresca, Sadie Frowne was part of the new immigration to the United States. Not quite seventeen in 1902, she still awaited marriage, success, and Americanization.

At age thirteen Frowne had come to the United States from Poland with her mother in search of greater economic opportunity. As with many immigrants, relatives supplied the capital to migrate—in this case, Frowne's Aunt Fanny. Mother and daughter traveled in steerage for twelve days before they could trade the dampness, crowding, sickness, and darkness of belowdecks for the beacon of the "Goddess of Liberty."

After working as a servant in New York City, Sadie Frowne entered a sweatshop as a garment worker. Soon after their arrival her mother died of tuberculosis—a disease so prevalent in the dense Jewish ghetto of New York City, the Lower East Side, that it became nicknamed "the Jewish Disease." Her mother had worked at the needles trade and Frowne hoped to learn a skill and go to school at night. In her first sweatshop, and later ones, she experienced sexual harassment from the men. A greenhorn garment worker could easily find herself the prey of male workers as well as the bosses, as Frowne discovered. Men joked about her physical qualities, and some touchd her when they passed. Although she was lucky enough to work in a shop that allowed her to keep her Saturday Sabbath—only a minority of Jewish workers could find such jobs—there were few other benefits. The pressure was enormous as the bosses accelerated the pace of work. Accidents were common, and, at the end of the day, six days a week, it was difficult to overcome fatigue. Again, however, she was lucky to work regularly. The garment business was seasonal and only a few workers could expect forty weeks of employment each year. The shops themselves rarely had any natural light or fresh air.

Independent, LIV (Sept. 25, 1902), 2279-82.

The safety hazards were notorious, although not until the Triangle Fire of 1911, when 146 workers, mostly young women, were killed, would conditions begin to change.

Frowne's Americanization took place rapidly. Through school and work she moved away from her traditional background. In 1900 she moved from the Lower East Side across the Brooklyn Bridge to Brownsville, a more "Americanized" Jewish quarter. She saved money, continued to go to school, and became sufficiently Americanized to expect to find in marriage emancipation from the sweatshops. Her fiancé, too, expected to leave the shops; he awaited a promised real estate job. While she was not completely Americanized, as evidenced by her visit to the fortune teller, she did not encounter anyone who seemed threatened by her traditional ways. Although firmly committed to her trade union, she assured her readers that she was no foreign radical such as a socialist or anarchist. Her union membership was an asset because unions in the early twentieth century sold themselves to American society as an important protector of native labor—they prevented the immigrant from selling his or her labor so cheaply as to depress the wage scale. Under these conditions, with the sweatshop being viewed as a temporary experience before marriage and childbearing, sweatshop work seemed bearable. But for many Jewish immigrant women, such as Sadie Frowne's mother, it meant work until an early death.

MY MOTHER was a tall, handsome, dark complexioned woman with red cheeks, large brown eyes and a great quantity of jet black, wavy hair. She was well educated, being able to talk in Russian, German, Polish and French, and even to read English print, tho, of course, she did not know what it meant. She kept a little grocer's shop in the little village where we lived at first. That was in Poland, somewhere on the frontier, and mother had charge of a gate between the countries, so that everybody who came through the gate had to show her a pass. She was much looked up to by the people, who used to come and ask her for advice. Her word was like law among them.

She had a wagon in which she used to drive about the country, selling her groceries, and sometimes she worked in the fields with my father.

For Jewish women immigrants from eastern Europe, there were few opportunities for work outside of the sweatshop. Photo by Lewis Hine. By permission of the International Museum of Photography at George Eastman House, Rochester, N.Y.

The grocer's shop was only one story high, and had one window, with very small panes of glass. We had two rooms behind it, and were happy while my father lived, altho we had to work very hard. By the time I was six years of age I was able to wash dishes and scrub floors, and by the time I was eight I attended to the shop while my mother was away driving her wagon or working in the fields with my father. She was strong and could work like a man./ 2/2/ /52

When I was a little more than ten years of age my father died. He was a good man and a steady worker, and we never knew what it was to be hungry while he lived. After he died troubles began, for the rent of our shop was about $6 a month and then there were food and clothes to provide. We needed little, it is true, but even soup, black bread and onions we could not always get.

We struggled along till I was nearly thirteen years of age and quite handy at housework and shop keeping, so far as I could learn them there. But we fell behind in the rent and mother kept thinking more and more that we should have to leave Poland and go across the sea to America where we heard it was much easier to make money. Mother wrote to Aunt Fanny, who lived in New York, and told her how hard it was to live in Poland, and Aunt Fanny advised her to come and bring me. I was out at service at this time and mother thought she would leave me— as I had a good place— and come to this country alone, sending for me afterward. But Aunt Fanny would not hear of this. She said we should both come at once, and she went around among our relatives in New York and took up a subscription for our passage.

We came by steerage on a steamship in a very dark place that smelt dreadfully. There were hundreds of other people packed in with us, men, women and children, and almost all of them were sick. It took us twelve days to cross the sea, and we thought we should die, but at last the voyage was over, and we came up and saw the beautiful bay and the big woman with the spikes on her head and the lamp that is lighted at night in her hand (Goddess of Liberty).

Aunt Fanny and her husband met us at the gate of this country and were very good to us, and soon I had a place to live out (domestic servant), while my mother got work in a factory making white goods.

I was only a little over thirteen years of age and a greenhorn, so I received $9 a month and board and lodging, which I thought was doing well. Mother, who, as I have said, was very clever, made $9 a week on white goods, which means all sorts of underclothing, and is high class work.

But mother had a very gay disposition. She liked to go around and see everything, and friends took her about New York at night and she caught a bad cold and coughed and coughed. She really had hasty consumption, but she didn't know it, and I didn't know it, and she tried to keep on working, but it was no use. She had not the strength. Two doctors attended her, but they could do nothing, and at last she died and I was left alone. I had saved money while out at service, but mother's sickness and funeral swept it all away and now I had to begin all over again.

Aunt Fanny had always been anxious for me to get an education, as I did not know how to read or write, and she thought that was wrong. Schools are different in Poland from what they are in this country, and I was always too busy to learn to read and write. So when mother died I thought I would try to learn a trade and then I could go to school at night and learn to speak the English language well.

So I went to work in Allen street (Manhattan) in what they call a sweatshop, making skirts by machine. I was new at the work and the foreman scolded me a great deal.

"Now, then," he would say, "this place is not for you to be looking around in. Attend to your work. That is what you have to do."

I did not know at first that you must not look around and talk, and I made many mistakes with the sewing, so that I was often called a "stupid animal." But I made $4 a week by working six days in the week. For there are two Sabbaths here—our own Sabbath, that comes on a Saturday, and the Christian Sabbath that comes on Sunday. It is against our law to work on our own Sabbath, so we work on their Sabbath.

In Poland I and my father and mother used to go to the synagogue on the Sabbath, but here the women don't go to the synagogue much, tho the men do. They are shut up working hard all the week long and when the Sabbath comes they like to sleep long in bed and afterward they must go out where they can breathe the air. The rabbis are strict here, but not so strict as in the old country.

I lived at this time with a girl named Ella, who worked in the same

factory and made $5 a week. We had the room all to ourselves, paying
$1.50 a week for it, and doing light housekeeping. It was in Allen
street, and the window looked out of the back, which was good,
because there was an elevated railroad in front, and in summer time a
great deal of dust and dirt came in at the front windows. We were on
the fourth story and could see all that was going on in the back rooms
of the houses behind us, and early in the morning the sun used to come
in our window.

We did our cooking on an oil stove, and lived well, as this list of our
expenses for one week will show:

ELLA AND SADIE FOR FOOD (ONE WEEK)

Tea	$0.06
Cocoa	.10
Bread and rolls	.40
Canned vegatables	.20
Potatoes	.10
Milk	.21
Fruit	.20
Butter	.15
Meat	.60
Fish	.15
Laundry	.25
Total	$2.42
Add rent	1.50
Grand total	$3.92

Of course, we could have lived cheaper, but we are both fond of
good things and felt that we could afford them.

We paid 18 cents for a half-pound of tea so as to get it good, and it
lasted us three weeks, because we had cocoa for breakfast. We paid 5
cents for six rolls and 5 cents a loaf for bread, which was the best
quality. Oatmeal cost us 10 cents for three and one-half pounds, and
we often had it in the morning, or Indian meal porridge in the place of
it, costing about the same. Half a dozen eggs cost about 13 cents on an
average, and we could get all the meat we wanted for a good hearty
meal for 20 cents—two pounds of chops, or a steak, or a bit of veal, or
a neck of lamb—something like that. Fish included butter fish,
porgies, codfish and smelts, averaging about 8 cents a pound.

Some people who buy at the last of the market, when the men with the carts want to go home, can get things very cheap, but they are likely to be stale, and we did not often do that with fish, fresh vegetables, fruit, milk or meat. Things that kept well we did buy that way and got good bargains. I got thirty potatoes for 10 cents one time, tho generally I could not get more than 15 of them for that amount. Tomatoes, onions and cabbages, too, we bought that way and did well, and we found a factory where we could buy the finest broken crackers for 3 cents a pound, and another place where we got broken candy for 10 cents a pound. Our cooking was done on an oil stove, and the oil for the stove and the lamp cost us 10 cents a week.

It cost me $2 a week to live, and I had a dollar a week to spend on clothing and pleasure, and saved the other dollar. I went to night school, but it was hard work learning at first as I did not know much English.

Two years ago I came to this place, Brownsville, where so many of my people are, and where I have friends. I got work in a factory making underskirts—all sorts of cheap underskirts, like cotton and calico for the summer and woolen for the winter, but never the silk, satin or velvet underskirts. I earned $4.50 a week and lived on $2 a week, the same as before.

I got a room in the house of some friends who lived near the factory. I pay $1 a week for the room and am allowed to do light housekeeping—that is, cook my meals in it. I get my own breakfast in the morning, just a cup of coffee and a roll, and at noon time I come home to dinner and take a plate of soup and a slice of bread with the lady of the house. My food for a week costs a dollar, just as it did in Allen street, and I have the rest of my money to do as I like with. I am earning $5.50 a week now, and will probably get another increase soon.

It isn't piecework in our factory, but one is paid by the amount of work done just the same. So it is like piecework. All the hands get different amounts, some as low as $3.50 and some of the men as high as $16 a week. The factory is in the third story of a brick building. It is in a room twenty feet long and fourteen broad. There are fourteen machines in it. I and the daughter of the people with whom I live work two of these machines. The other operators are all men, some young and some old.

At first a few of the young men were rude. When they passed me they would touch my hair and talk about my eyes and my red cheeks, and make jokes. I cried and said that if they did not stop I would leave the place. The boss said that that should not be, that no one must annoy me. Some of the other men stood up for me, too, especially Henry, who said two or three times that he wanted to fight. Now the men all treat me very nicely. It was just that some of them did not know better, not being educated.

Henry is tall and dark, and he has a small mustache. His eyes are brown and large. He is pale and much educated, having been to school. He knows a great many things and has some money saved. I think nearly $400. He is not going to be in a sweatshop all the time, but will soon be in the real estate business, for a lawyer that knows him well has promised to open an office and pay him to manage it.

Henry has seen me home every night for a long time and makes love to me. He wants me to marry him, but I am not seventeen yet, and I think that is too young. He is only nineteen, so we can wait.

I have been to the fortune teller's three or four times, and she always tells me that tho I have had such a lot of trouble I am to be very rich and happy. I believe her because she has told so many things that have come true. So I will keep on working in the factory for a time. Of course it is hard, but I would have to work hard even if I was married.

I get up at half-past five o'clock every morning and make myself a cup of coffee on the oil stove. I eat a bit of bread and perhaps some fruit and then go to work. Often I get there soon after six o'clock so as to be in good time, tho the factory does not open till seven. I have heard that there is a sort of clock that calls you at the very time you want to get up, but I can't believe that because I don't see how the clock would know.

At seven o'clock we all sit down to our machines and the boss brings to each one the pile of work that he or she is to finish during the day, what they call in English their "stint." This pile is put down beside the machine and as soon as a skirt is done it is laid on the other side of the machine. Sometimes the work is not all finished by six o'clock and then the one who is behind must work overtime. Sometimes one is finished ahead of time and gets away at four or five o'clock, but generally we are not done till six o'clock.

The machines go like mad all day, because the faster you work the more money you get. Sometimes in my haste I get my finger caught and the needle goes right through it. It goes so quick tho, that it does not hurt much. I bind the finger up with a piece of cotton and go on working. We all have accidents like that. Where the needle goes through the nail it makes a sore figner, or where it splinters a bone it does much harm. Sometimes a finger has to come off. Generally, tho, one can be cured by a salve.

All the time we are working the boss walks about examining the finished garments and making us do them over again if they are not just right. So we have to be careful as well as swift. But I am getting so good at the work that within a year I will be making $7 a week, and then I can save at least $3.50 a week. I have over $200 saved now.

The machines are all run by foot power, and at the end of the day one feels so weak that there is a great temptation to lie right down and sleep. But you must go out and get air, and have some pleasure. So instead of lying down I go out, generally with Henry. Sometimes we go to Coney Island, where there are good dancing places, and sometimes we go to Ulmer Park to picnics. I am very fond of dancing, and, in fact, all sorts of pleasure. I go to the theater quite often, and like those plays that make you cry a great deal. "The Two Orphans" is good. Last time I saw it I cried all night because of the hard times that the children had in the play. I am going to see it again when it comes here.

For the last two winters I have been going to night school at Public School 84 on Glenmore avenue. I have learned reading, writing and arithmetic. I can read quite well in English now and I look at the newspapers every day. I read English books, too, sometimes. The last one that I read was "A Mad Marriage," by Charlotte Braeme. She's a grand writer and makes things just like real to you. You feel as if you were the poor girl yourself going to get married to a rich duke.

I am going back to night school again this winter. Plenty of my friends go there. Some of the women in my class are more than forty years of age. Like me, they did not have a chance to learn anything in the old country. It is good to have an education; it makes you feel higher. Ignorant peole are all low. People say now that I am clever and fine in conversation.

We have just finished a strike in our business. It spread all over and the United Brotherhood of Garment Workers was in it. That takes in the cloakmakers, coatmakers, and all the others. We struck for shorter hours, and after being out four weeks won the fight. We only have to work nine and a half hours a day and we get the same pay as before. So the union does good after all in spite of what some people say against it—that it just takes our money and does nothing.

I pay 25 cents a month to the union, but I do not begrudge that because it is for our benefit. The next strike is going to be for a raise of wages, which we all ought to have. But tho I belong to the union I am not a Socialist or an Anarchist. I don't know exactly what those things mean. There is a little expense for charity, too. If any worker is injured or sick we all give money to help.

Some of the women blame me very much because I spend so much money on clothes. They say that instead of a dollar a week I ought not to spend more than twenty-five cents a week on clothes, and that I should save the rest. But a girl must have clothes if she is to go into high society at Ulmer Park or Coney Island or the theatre. Those who blame me are the old country people who have old-fashioned notions, but the people who have been here a long time know better. A girl who does not dress well is stuck in a corner, even if she is pretty, and Aunt Fanny says that I do just right to put on plenty of style.

I have many friends and we often have jolly parties. Many of the young men like to talk to me, but I don't go out with any except Henry.

Lately he has been urging me more and more to get married—but I think I'll wait.

Brooklyn, N.Y.

Women on the Farm

Although we know little about the process that led to the writing and publication of these brief autobiographies, it is clear that "One Farmer's Wife" differs from nearly all of the others. It was a self-consciously motivated literary effort. The original essay on which the final autobiography was based had been written in a correspondence school course. The *Independent* returned the essay to the Illinois woman; apparently she satisfied their editorial demands, for in 1905 the revised text was printed. The *Independent*, in paying the author, hoped that the fee would not encourage her literary career at the expense of "her domestic duties."

"One Farmer's Wife" is the story of an unfulfilled, unhappy woman. Although she expressed great pride in her children, her marriage was an unsuccessful one. She had pledged herself to her future husband when she had been quite young, but after earning a teacher's certificate at age eighteen, she wished to break her promise. He would not release her, and she married him. For six years she ran the home and garden and helped him to farm as well; she then had two children, and added childrearing to her other duties.

Combining household and farm work required great endurance. The farmer's wife described a typical May day. Rising at 4 A.M., she started a fire, tended the garden, fed the children, made up her husband's dinner pail, herded the cows, fed the chickens, then returned inside for domestic chores, supervised the children, tended the garden again, made dinner, and continued working the rest of the day alternating between inside and outside labor. She did not receive the same satisfaction from manual work that her husband did, and she disliked many of the duties, especially the domestic ones. It is clear that she would have preferred formal education and reading and writing, but her husband—indeed any farmer—could not manage alone, and her labor was required on the farm.

"One Farmer's Wife," *Independent*, LVIII (Feb. 9, 1905), 294-99, and "Women on the Farm," *Independent*, LVIII (Mar. 9, 1905), 549-54.

The inability of the farmer's wife to pursue her own interests led to unhappiness and frustration. An important theme underlying the entire essay is the conflict between husband and wife, which in the early years of their marriage had been resolved exclusively in favor of the husband. It was the husband's miserliness that ruled, his desire to accumulate money for its own sake rather than for its purchasing power. Although the wife loved to read, they began to receive a newspaper only after nearly a decade of marriage; he judged it a waste of money, and until then she lacked the courage to stand up to him. Finally, when she convinced him to allow her to take a correspondence course, he consented only after being persuaded that her earnings as a writer might justify speculation in tuition. As it was, she had to agree to give up her magazine subscriptions in return for taking the course.

The title of the article symbolized the wife's complaint: "One Farmer's Wife." Nowhere is her name even hinted at. In essence, she told the reader that she was defined as a person only through her husband. More important, she grudgingly accepted her husband's dominant role, and only in later years had she developed the courage to begin to stand up to him and fight for her independent existence and identity. This is a rare social document, providing a window through which to view the most private and discreet of American institutions: the family, and husband-wife relations within it.

The wife was announcing her unhappiness to the *Independent*'s audience. In doing so she reflected the increasingly independent status of women; possibly she was influenced by the strong voices raised by feminists at the turn of the century. To feel unhappy in itself was a progressive step; it meant that she felt she had a right to be happy. As she fought to become involved in literature, she was engaging in a sphere totally unrelated to the farm and occupying an area that her husband could not share at all. Clearly this represented an important independent step, one that had to be defended to her husband as long as they remained married.

Reflecting her public discussion of unhappiness on the farm and in marriage and husband-wife conflict, "One Farmer's Wife" was the most controversial of all of the autobiographies published by the *Independent*. She had touched exposed nerves among both satisfied and dissatisfied farm women, and they rushed to add their voices to the debate. A selection from these responses was printed in "Women on the Farm." Not all of the *Independent*'s correspondents understood the underlying issue, but "One Farmer's Wife" opened the pages of this weekly to issues rarely discussed openly in American society.

I HAVE BEEN a farmer's wife in one of the States of the Middle West for thirteen years, and everybody knows that the farmer's wife must of a necessity be a very practical woman, if she would be a successful one.

I am not a practical woman and consequently have been accounted a failure by practical friends and especially by my husband, who is wholly practical.

We are told that the mating of people of opposite natures promotes intellectuality in the offspring; but I think that happy homes are of more consequence than extreme precocity of children. However, I believe that people who are thinking of mating do not even consider whether it is to be the one or the other.

We do know that when people of opposite tastes get married there's a discordant note runs through their entire married life. It's only a question of which one has the stronger will in determining which taste shall predominate.

In our case my husband has the stronger will; he is innocent of book learning, is a natural hustler who believes that the only way to make an honest living lies in digging it out of the ground, so to speak, and being a farmer, he finds plenty of digging to do; he has an inherited tendency to be miserly, loves money for its own sake rather than for its purchasing power, and when he has it in his possession he is loath to part with it, even for the most necessary articles, and prefers to eschew hired help in every possible instance that what he does make may be his very own.

No man can run a farm without some one to help him, and in this case I have always been called upon and expected to help do anything that a man would be expected to do; I began this when we were first married, when there were few household duties and no reasonable excuse for refusing to help.

I was reared on a farm, was healthy and strong, was ambitious, and the work was not disagreeable, and having no children for the first six years of married life, the habit of going whenever asked to became firmly fixed, and he had no thought of hiring a man to help him, since I could do anything for which he needed help.

I was always religiously inclined; brought up to attend Sunday school, not in a haphazard way, but to attend every Sunday all the year round, and when I was twelve years old I was appointed teacher to a Sunday school class, a position I proudly held until I married at eighteen years of age.

I was an apt student at school and before I was eighteen I had earned a teacher's certificate of the second grade and would gladly have remained in school a few more years, but I had, unwittingly, agreed to marry the man who is now my husband, and tho I begged to be released, his will was so much the stronger that I was unable to free myself without wounding a loving heart, and could not find it in my heart to do so.

All through life I have found my dislike for giving offense to be my undoing. When we were married and moved away from my home church, I fain would have adopted the church of my new residence, but my husband did not like to go to church; had rather go visiting on Sundays, and, rather than have my right hand give offense, I cut it off.

I always had a passion for reading; during girlhood it was along educational lines; in young womanhood it was for love stories, which remained ungratified because my father thought it sinful to read stories of any kind, and especially love stories.

Later, when I was married, I borrowed everything I could find in the line of novels and stories, and read them by stealth still, for my husband thought it a willful waste of time to read anything and that it showed a lack of love for him if I would rather read than to talk to him when I had a few moments of leisure, and, in order to avoid giving offense and still gratify my desire, I would only read when he was not at the house, thereby greatly curtailing my already too limited reading hours.

In reading miscellaneously I got glimpses now and then of the great poets and authors, which aroused a great desire for a thorough perusal of them all; but up till the present time I have not been permitted to satisfy this desire. As the years have rolled on there has been more work and less leisure until it is only by the greatest effort that I may read current news.

It is only during the last three years that I have had the news to read, for my husband is so very penurious that he would never consent to subscribing for papers of any kind and that old habit of avoiding that which would give offense was so fixed that I did not dare to break it.

The addition of two children to our family never altered or interfered with the established order of things to any appreciable extent. My strenuous outdoor life agreed with me, and even when my children were born I was splendidly prepared for the ordeal and made rapid recovery. I still hoed and tended the truck patches and garden, still watered the stock and put out feed for them, still went to the hay field and helped harvest and house the bounteous crops; still helped harvest the golden grain later on when the cereals ripened; often took one team and dragged ground to prepare the seed-bed for wheat for weeks at the time, while my husband was using the other team on another farm which he owns several miles away.

While the children were babies they were left at the house, and when they were larger they would go with me to my work; now they are large enough to help a little during the summer and to go to school in winter; they help a great deal during the fruit canning season—in fact, can and do work at almost everything, pretty much as I do.

All the season, from the coming in of the first fruits until the making of mincemeat at Christmas time, I put up canned goods for future use; gather in many bushels of field beans and the other crops usually raised on the farm; make sourkraut, ketchup, pickles, etc.

This is a vague, general idea of how I spend my time; my work is so varied that it would be difficult, indeed, to describe a typical day's work.

Any bright morning in the latter part of May I am out of bed at four o'clock; next, after I have dressed and combed my hair, I start a fire in the kitchen stove, and while the stove is getting hot I go to my flower garden and gather a choice, half-blown rose and a spray of bride's wreath, and arrange them in my hair, and sweep the floors and then cook breakfast.

While the other members of the family are eating breakfast I strain away the morning's milk (for my husband milks the cows while I get breakfast), and fill my husband's dinner-pail, for he will go to work on our other farm for the day.

By this time it is half-past five o'clock, my husband is gone to his work, and the stock loudly pleading to be turned into the pastures. The younger cattle, a half-dozen steers, are left in the pasture at night, and I now drive the two cows a half-quarter mile and turn them in with the others, come back, and then there's a horse in the barn that belongs in a field where there is no water, which I take to a spring quite a distance from the barn; bring it back and turn it into a field with the sheep, a dozen in number, which are housed at night.

The young calves are then turned out into the warm sunshine, and the stock hogs, which are kept in a pen, are clamoring for feed, and I carry a pailful of swill to them, and hasten to the house and turn out the chickens and put out feed and water for them, and it is, perhaps, 6.30 a.m.

I have not eaten breakfast yet, but that can wait; I make the beds next and straighten things up in the living room, for I dislike to have the early morning caller find my house topsy-turvy. When this is done I go to the kitchen, which also serves as a dining-room, and uncover the table, and take a mouthful of food occasionally as I pass to and fro at my work until my appetite is appeased.

By the time the work is done in the kitchen it is about 7.15 a.m., and the cool morning hours have flown, and no hoeing done in the garden yet, and the children's toilet has to be attended to and churning has to be done.

Finally the children are washed and churning done, and it is eight o'clock, and the sun getting hot, but no matter, weeds die quickly when cut down in the heat of the day, and I use the hoe to a good advantage until the dinner hour, which is 11.30 a.m. We come in, and I comb my hair, and put fresh flowers in it, and eat a cold dinner, put out feed and water for the chickens; set a hen, perhaps, sweep the floors again; sit down and rest, and read a few moments, and it is nearly one o'clock, and I sweep the door yard while I am waiting for the clock to strike the hour.

I make and sow a flower bed, dig around some shrubbery, and go back to the garden to hoe until time to do the chores at night, but ere long some hogs come up to the back gate, through the wheat field, and when I go to see what is wrong I find that the cows have torn the fence down, and they, too, are in the wheat field.

With much difficulty I get them back into their own domain and repair the fence. I hoe in the garden till four o'clock; then I go into the house and get supper, and prepare something for the dinner pail tomorrow; when supper is all ready it is set aside, and I pull a few hundred plants of tomato, sweet potato or cabbage for transplanting, set them in a cool, moist place where they will not wilt, and I then go after the horse, water him, and put him in the barn; call the sheep and house them, and go after the cows and milk them, feed the hogs, put down hay for three horses, and put oats and corn in their troughs and set those plants and come in and fasten up the chickens, and it is dark. By this time it is 8 o'clock p.m.; my husband has come home, and we are eating supper; when we are through eating I make the beds ready, and the children and their father go to bed, and I wash the dishes and get things in shape to get breakfast quickly next morning.

It is now about 9 o'clock p.m., and after a short prayer I retire for the night.

As a matter of course, there's hardly two days together which require the same routine, yet every day is as fully occupied in some way or other as this one, with varying tasks as the seasons change. In early spring we are planting potatoes, making plant beds, planting garden, early corn patches, setting strawberries, planting corn, melons, cow peas, sugar cane, beans, popcorn, peanuts, etc.

Oats are sown in March and April, but I do not help do that, because the ground is too cold.

Later in June we harvest clover hay, in July timothy hay, and in August pea hay.

Winter wheat is ready to harvest the latter part of June, and oats the middle of July.

These are the main crops, supplemented by cabbages, melons, potatoes, tomatoes, etc.

Fully half of my time is devoted to helping my husband, more than half during the active work season, and not that much during the winter months; only a very small portion of my time is devoted to reading. My reading matter accumulates during the week, and I think I will stay at home on Sunday and read, but as we have many visitors on Sunday I am generally disappointed.

I sometimes visit my friends on Sunday because they are so insistent that I should, tho I would prefer spending the day reading quietly at home. I have never had a vacation, but if I should be allowed one I should certainly be pleased to spend it in an art gallery.

As winter draws nigh I make snug all the vegetables and apples, pumpkins, and such things as would damage by being frozen, and gather in the various kinds of nuts which grow in our woods, to eat during the long, cold winter.

My husband's work keeps him away from home during the day all the winter, except in extremely inclement weather, and I feed and water the stock, which have been brought in off the pastures; milk the cows and do all the chores which are to be done about a farm in winter.

By getting up early and hustling around pretty lively I do all this and countless other things; keep house in a crude, simple manner; wash, make and mend our clothes; make rag carpets, cultivate and keep more flowers than anybody in the neighborhood, raise some chickens to sell and some to keep, and even teach instrumental music sometimes.

I have always had an itching to write, and, with all my multitudinous cares, I have written, in a fitful way, for several papers, which do not pay for such matter, just because I was pleased to see my articles in print.

I have a long list of correspondents, who write regularly and often to me, and, by hook and crook, I keep up with my letter-writing, for, next to reading, I love to write and receive letters, tho my husband says I will break him up buying so much writing material; when, as a matter of course, I pay for it out of my own scanty income.

I am proud of my children, and have, from the time they were young babies, tried to make model children of them. They were not spoiled as some babies are, and their education was begun when I first began to speak to them, with the idea of not having the work to do over later on. True, they did not learn to spell until they were old enough to start to school, because I did not have time to teach them that; but, in going about my work, I told them stories of all kinds, in plain, simple language which they could understand, and after once hearing a story they could repeat it in their own way, which did not differ greatly from mine, to any one who cared to listen, for they were not timid or afraid of anybody.

I have watched them closely, and never have missed an opportunity to correct their errors until their language is as correct as that of the average adult, as far as their vocabulary goes, and I have tried to make it as exhaustive as my time would permit.

I must admit that there is very little time for the higher life for myself, but my soul cries out for it, and my heart is not in my homely duties; they are done in a mechanical, abstracted way, not worthy of a woman of high ambitions; but my ambitions are along other lines.

I do not mean to say that I have no ambition to do my work well, and to be a model housekeeper, for I would scorn to slight my work intentionally; it is just this way: There are so many outdoor duties that the time left for household duties is so limited that I must rush through them, with a view to getting each one done in the shortest possible time, in order to get as many things accomplished as possible, for there is never time to do half as much as needs to be done.

All the time that I have been going about this work I have been thinking of things I have read; of things I have on hand to read when I can get time, and of other things which I have a desire to read, but cannot hope to while the present condition exists.

As a natural consequence, there are, daily, numerous instances of absentmindedness on my part; many things left undone that I really could have done, by leaving off something else of less importance, if I had not forgotten the thing of the more importance. My husband never fails to remind me that it is caused by my reading so much; that I would get along much better if I should never see a book or paper, while really I would be distracted if all reading matter was taken from me.

I use an old fashioned churn, and the process of churning occupies from thirty minutes to three hours, according to the condition of the cream, and I always read something while churning, and tho that may look like a poor way to attain self-culture, yet if your reading is of the nature to bring about that desirable result, one will surely be greatly benefited by these daily exercises.

But if one is just reading for amusement, they might read a great deal more than that and not derive any great benefit; but my reading has always been for the purpose of becoming well informed; and when knitting stockings for the family I always have a book or paper in reading distance; or, if I have a moment to rest or to wait on something, I pick up something and read during the time. I even take a paper with me to the fields and read while I stop for rest.

I often hear ladies remark that they do not have time to read. I happen to know that they have a great deal more time that I do, but not having any burning desire to read, the time is spent in some other way; often spent at a neighbor's house gossiping about the other neighbors.

I suppose it is impossible for a woman to do her best at everything which she would like to do, but I really would like to. I almost cut sleep out of my routine in trying to keep up all the rows which I have started in on; in the short winter days I just get the cooking and house straightening done in addition to looking after the stock and poultry, and make a garment occasionally, and wash and iron the clothes; all the other work is done after night by lamp light, and when the work for the day is over, or at least the most pressing part of it, and the family are all asleep and no one to forbid it, I spend a few hours writing or reading.

The minister who performed the marriage ceremony for us has always taken a kindly interest in our fortunes and, knowing of my literary bent, has urged me to turn it to account; but there seemed to be so little time and opportunity that I could not think seriously of it, altho I longed for a literary career; but my education had been dropped for a dozen years or more, and I knew that I was not properly equipped for that kind of a venture.

This friend was so insistent that I was induced to compete for a prize in a short story contest in a popular magazine not long since, tho I entered it fully prepared for a failure.

About that time there came in my way the literature of a correspondence school which would teach, among other things, short story writing by mail; it set forth all the advantages of a literary career, and proposed properly to equip its students in that course for a consideration.

This literature I greedily devoured, and felt that I could not let the opportunity slip, tho I despaired of getting my husband's consent.

I presented the remunerative side of it to him, but he could only see the expense of taking the course, and wondered how I could find time to spend in the preparation, even if it should be profitable in the end;

but he believed it was all a humbug; that they would get my money and I would hear from them no more.

When I had exhausted my arguments to no avail, I sent my literary friend to him, to try his persuasive powers. The two of us, finally, gained his consent, but it was on condition that the venture was to be kept profoundly secret, for he felt sure that there would be nothing but failure, and he desired that no one should know of it and have cause for ridicule.

Contrary to his expectations, the school has proven very trust-worthy, and I am in the midst of a course of instruction which is very pleasing to me; and I find time for study and exercises between the hours of eight and eleven at night, when the family are asleep and quiet. I am instructed to read a great deal, with a certain purpose in view, but that is impossible since I had to promise my husband that I would drop all my papers, periodicals, etc., on which I was paying out money for subscriptions before he would consent to my taking the course. This I felt willing to do, that I might prepare myself for more congenial tasks; I hope to accomplish something worthy of note in a literary way since I have been a failure in all other pursuits. One cannot be anything in particular as long as they try to be everything, and my motto has always been: "Strive to Excel," and it has caused worry wrinkles to mar my countenance, because I could not, under the circumstances, excel in any particular thing.

I have a few friends who are so anxious for my success that they are having certain publications of reading matter sent to me at their own expense; however, there's only a very limited number who know of my ambitions.

My friends have always been so kind not to hint that I had not come up to their expectations in various lines, but I inwardly knew that they regarded me as a financial failure; they knew that my husband would not allow the money that was made off the farm to be spent on the family, but still they knew of other men who did the same, yet the wives managed some way to have money of their own and to keep up the family expenses and clothe themselves and children nicely anyhow, but they did not seem to take into account that these thrifty wives had that time all for their own in which to earn a livelihood while my time was demanded by my husband, to be spent in doing things for him which would contribute to the general proceeds of the farm, yet would add nothing to my income, since I was supposed to look to my own resources for my spending money.

When critical housewives spend the day with me I always feel that my surroundings appear to a disadvantage. They cannot possibly know the inside workings of our home, and knowing myself to be capable of the proper management of a home if I had the chance of others, I feel like I am receiving a mental criticism from them which is unmerited, and when these smart neighbors tell me proudly how many young chicks they have, and how many eggs and old hens they have sold during the year, I am made to feel that they are crowing over their shrewdness, which they regard as lacking in me, because they will persist in measuring my opportunities by their own.

I might add that the neighbors among whom I live are illiterate and unmusical, and that my redeeming qualities, in their eyes, are my superior education and musical abilities; they are kind enough to give me more than justice on these qualities because they are poor judges of such matters.

But money is king, and if I might turn my literary bent to account, and surround myself with the evidences of prosperity, I may yet hope fully to redeem myself in their eyes, and I know that I will have attained my ambition in that line.

Illinois

LETTERS

Shortly after my graduation from a "freshwater" college for women, five years ago, I found myself in the following circumstances: Through changes in family affairs I was left with myself and an invalid sister to support. My assets were as follows: A farm of two hundred acres, with an average amount of stock and farming tools, and a farmhouse that had been enlarged and remodeled and used for the past few years as a summer boarding house. This property was situated in southern Massachusetts, two miles from a village, and was genuine, simon-pure country. The farm was adorned with a $5000 mortgage, bearing 5 per cent. interest; the whole plant under a forced sale would not have realized more than $10,000, which would have supplied a possible $250 a year income for the support of two persons. So much for the farm situation.

I had offered me an assistant teacher's position at my *Alma Mater* with a $600 salary, but this made no provision for my sister. Also I had a great prejudice against teaching for women, having seen numerous nervous wrecks after five years at this work.

Matrimony seemed unavailable for the moment, from lack of inclination on my part, or on that of any one else, for that matter; so this was dismissed.

A possible position, as bookkeeper or in any of the allied occupations would have entailed a course at a business college, and I had only a few hundred dollars as capital.

Considering all things, I decided on the farm. So, with many misgivings, I began active operation there March 1st, 1900. The place had been in charge of the owner of the adjoining property for a year. He had worked it on the share arrangement and the house had been closed. My first act was to hire as foreman an Irishman, thirty years old, who, with his family, was installed in a small cottage on the place. His wages are $30 a month, rent free, and he takes his meals at the house. He hired his own assistants, two young men of the same nationality. These men get $23 a month and their board. They have proved honest and trustworthy servants. I have never had to change them. I go on the principle that a little nagging goes a long way, and my experience with farm help proves it a good one.

At the beginning of my enterprise there was a herd of twenty grade cows on the farm, and the milk was sold to a man who peddled it in a manufacturing town five miles away. He called for the milk once a day and paid 3 cents per quart for it. This arrangement was continued for six months, when a sanitarium being opened in the village, where fifty patients were cared for, I secured the contract to supply this institution with milk at 5¼ cents a quart, the milk to be delivered twice a day. The sanitarium was two miles from the farm. This contract is still in force, the sanitarium has grown until it now has a hundred patients, and the milk bills for the past year foot $2,558.04. Gradually I have worked up a retail milk trade along the way to the sanitarium and in this way sell about thirty quarts of milk a day at 6 cents a quart. One man regularly delivers the milk, keeping account of it on a milk sheet, which he hands in to me the first of every month and from which I make the bills. The milkman also has entire care of his cans and wagon.

I have put up two of the Williams Company's silos, one eighteen feet and one sixteen feet in diameter. The ensilage gives excellent satisfaction, bringing the cows through the winter in good condition. This ensilage food is balanced with a ration of hay, wheat midlings and gluten or cotton-seed meal. This winter the herd numbers thirty cows.

To return to the beginning of my work: I decided to take boarders, since the house was arranged for that purpose and much too large for ordinary use with its accommodations for twenty guests. I first hired a Nova Scotia woman as cook and her daughter as general assistant at $18 and $12 a month. With their help I put the house in order, papering ten rooms myself. The place was entirely furnished, and I made only some minor repairs that spring. In filling my house the first year a great deal of help was received from persons engaged in the same business in the village already mentioned, which is quite a summer resort. They were kind enough to turn their overflow in my direction, and since getting fairly established my patrons have done my advertising. People come into the country nowadays earlier than they used to and stay later. The house is usually well filled from the middle of May until late in October. I charge from $9 to $12 a week for board, the average price being about $10. I have always done everything possible to encourage people to bring children here. The farm life is just the thing for them and, of course, my place entirely lacks the "resort" attractions which appeal to young people. Special attention has always been paid to the table to make the fare, tho simple, abundant and the best of its kind. The foreman is an excellent gardener and I am able to serve my guests with fresh vegetables of all kinds, raising also quantities of delicious strawberries, raspberries and currants. People are very appreciative of these things. Milk and cream are had in plenty from the farm herd. No butter is made on the place, but is furnished by a nearby dairyman. The farm is fortunate in being suppled by a unfailing spring of pure water, which runs to the house of its own power and in quantities sufficient for all uses. Marketing is done in the usual country system of carts driving about and the service is good; groceries are bought chiefly at a New York wholesale house.

I make it a practice to be on the place all the morning. In summer I am up and dressed by half-past six. By this time the early breakfast for the men and maids has been served and eaten, and I go out with the foreman to plan the work for the day, leaving him to give the orders to his assistants. I look over the barn and stable often to see that all the animals look well and contented. Six horses are kept to do the farm work and to rent to the guests in the house for driving. Some of these horses are excellent roadsters, and all help cheerfully about the farm work. They are well fed and nothing unreasonable is asked of them, kindness to all the animals being one of the first rules of the place.

But I am staying too long out of doors; even if the lovely summer morning is tempting I must go in and superintend the eight o'clock breakfast for my guests. When this is over the other meals for the day are planned; a regular weekly bill of fare is never used. Having acquired, by inheritance and study, considerable knack as a cook, I always prepare certain dishes myself, such as desserts, salads and made meat dishes. Through the summer two extra women servants are hired in addition to the two employed the year around. I find no trouble in keeping busy about the house until the one o'clock dinner. In the afternoon there are often errands to do or a trip to be made to the town five miles away, where shopping is done. Walking is a great pleasure and few days in the year pass without my spending an hour or two in this recreation. Most women living in the country do not walk enough; nothing horrifies them more than a suggestion of walking three or four miles. I go often in the fields, partly to avoid constant offers of "a ride" from kindly neighbors, whose greeting usually is, "What's the matter with all your horses?" as tho no one would ever walk who could possibly avoid it. I am devoted to the life of the fields and woods and am a keen botanist.

I am often asked what there can be for the three men to do on the farm all winter. The care of the cows takes much more time during this season, when they are in the stable, than when they are at pasture in summer. Then there are thirty cords of wood to be chopped and worked up, for we use nothing else for fuel, burning great four-foot logs in the furnace, cooking with wood, and supplying the six open fireplaces with plenty of birch and hickory logs. This work, considering the short and often stormy days, seems to keep all busy.

As for boasting of having grown rich in the past five years, I am afraid that is impossible. I have kept up the place in good order and made some permanent repairs at a cost of about $500 a year, supported my sister and myself, paid all bills and wages promptly, and have put $500 in a savings bank in case of a wet day. If I were like the people who write their experiences for the *Ladies' Home Journal,* the mortgage on the farm would doubtless have been paid off before this time. I am willing and, being perfectly well, am able to work hard, but I do not propose to deny myself the rational pleasures of life. Our home is made pleasant and comfortable, I buy books and subscribe to magazines and a New York daily paper. We subscribe to the library which the village boasts and which for $3 a year allows subscribers four books a week; also to the Tabard Inn Station in the town. The telephone connects us with the neighboring farmhouses and is a great help both in pleasure and business. In winter I mean to make two or three short trips to New York and an occasional one to Boston, and to dress well enough so that my friends in these places need not feel ashamed to see me come in. I am so much in love with country life that I feel out of place in the city, and after a short stay am thankful to get back to my own "neck of the woods."

I keep an accurate cash account of all receipts and disbursements, and in glancing through this for the past year I see that my receipts from boarders were $3,157. All the productiveness of the farm goes to maintain the dairy, for besides the $2,900 received for milk and cream I see only $150 for potatoes and $120 for pork sold. The expenses are necessarily heavy. The wage item runs over $100 a month, and other items I notice are $135 for commercial fertilizer and seed; taxes, $106; interest on mortgage, $250; oats and feed, $500; fire insurance, $90. These, with daily running expenses, take the money about as fast as it comes in.

On the whole, mine seems a sane and pleasant course of life and I have never regretted the school teaching or other alternatives. It is some satisfaction to be "the boss," even if the domain is small.

A New England Woman Farmer

My heart was touched by the tale of wo told by the farmer's wife "Illinois" in your issue of February 9th, and fearing your readers might think that a majority or even many of the farmers' wives suffer like her I will give you my experience as a farmer's wife for the last 22 years. To begin, I am the daughter of Irish emigrants, who came to America as poor as English persecution could make them, and God knows that was poor enough, and settled in one of the valleys of the Alleghenies. I was not there, then, but came later. I did the usual chores about a farmhouse and went to the district school till I was fifteen years, when I was sent to school to a convent, from whence I came able to teach in the common schools. I taught in several counties, and every place I taught "Willie went a-wooing," but I seemed proof against Cupid's arrows. Even when the man who is now my husband wrote me an introductory letter I rejected him. He was almost a stranger to me and things went along as usual for two years when I accidentally met "John" again. I could not but admire "the man" in him and the candor and boldness with which he practiced his religion. I had read Burns:

> Conceal yoursel' as weel's ye can,
> Frae critical dissection,
> But keek through every other man
> Wi' sharpen'd sly inspection.

I never thought it well for a young lady to let love get the better of judgment. My young lady friends said to me, "Give that fellow a wide berth. He is too much of a buckwheat for you," but I listened to John, and you know when a woman listens what she will do. John "led me to the altar," and then led me to his home, over one hundred miles from "my native heath." When I arrived at his home I found he possessed a large farm, with many buildings and much stock, and work enough for a small army; and, like the husband of "Illinois," "he was a hustler." He had a strong will, and his word was law about the whole place. My heart sank. Everything was out of my line. I said to myself, "What can I do here?" But my husband's kindness came to the rescue. I found him not miserly or stingy, but right the opposite, caring not for money only as a means with which to accomplish his object. He laid all his plans before me, asked my opinion in everything he was about to do, and when I told him I knew nothing about it, he said it would teach me if he were called "off to yonder." I found such knowledge very useful at times when he was away from home. I would sally forth to see that things were aright. I found he had a good library, was a lover of books, from which I often had to take him at the midnight hour, and that when we "locked horns" on a literary subject I was often vanquished. I had some money from teaching with which I bought some new things for the house, and gave the balance to my husband to use in the improvements he was making. He put a wind mill over a well and pumped the water into a tank high in one of the barns. From there he piped it into the kitchen, bathroom, stock troughs, etc. He bought a new piano, as I had been taught to play some. I had learned to milk when at home, and often on Sunday evenings when the hired men would "play hookey" I would go to the barn and help John milk thirty cows, come to the house and play "Garry Owen" in a manner that would make a Rough Rider think of Cuba. When I ask John for money he doesn't lean back in his chair and say, "What did you do with the last fifty cents I gave you?" but gives me what I say I need, and never yet asked me what I did with it. I have never asked for a horse to go any place but it was ready, with a driver if I wanted one. We keep several horses, and John's motto is, "I keep the horses well fed and shod, and when we want to go they must." In all these years I have worked hard, but ever with a good will, always kept a house girl when we could get one, and was never asked to do anything I did not wish to do. When we were two years married a baby boy came to add his mite to the confusion, and they kept coming occasionally until we had five. We raised them tenderly; looked after the better part. When John hired a man he always put this in: "If I know of you being profane or obscene your time is up." As they grew older we sent them to the common school, thence to a high school and thence to a university, and altho they are the sons of a "farmer's bond servant," they have always distinguished themselves on the forum and gridiron. They were raised away from the allurements of city life, have no bad habits and have never brought a blush to my cheek. I know always just where my husband is. He is never at a "club house" and his wife pining at home. When he goes to any entertainment he takes his wife along. We don't believe in the wife raising chickens for pin money. We have no separate acts. Everything is in common, both in earning and spending. John thinks or says, at least, that the wife is "the whole thing" at the home, and so has always treated me as the principal partner in the business. I have tried to act my part along these lines and therefore there is no hitch. Now if I had the power and the will to be other than a farmer's wife, where could I better myself?

A Pennsylvania Woman

It seems to me that you have put us farmer folks in a wrong light in your last week's issue. . . . It seems to me "One Farmer's Wife" is not only unfortunate in her husband, but also in her place of residence. . . . having been a farmer's daughter 30 years, a farmer's wife 6 years, and having a varied experience from residence in Ohio, Colorado and Iowa, the article referred to reads, for the most part, like 20 years ago.

I did not suppose there was a farmer's wife in the United States to-day doing the family knitting. The most of us have learned that it is not economy to do this, or to make our husbands' clothes or launder their "biled" linen.

Some of my neighbors eat in their kitchens, but I could almost say that every wife has a cream separator, a patent churn and other labor-saving devices. Some of them "do not have time" for solid reading, but most homes (particularly since having R. F. D.) have the daily paper and several good magazines. And, yes, we have some gossips. Don't you have them in town, too?

We *do* work hard and long (but so do our husbands), and I am honestly grateful for your sympathy. I smiled a trifle bitterly the other day as I wondered if Mrs. Ashby-Macfadyen didn't know that "housekeeping is genuinely hard work" for thousands of her American sisters, too. I have never feared that I should rust out. I am busy, busy, and must be quick and methodical or be swamped. But when I am wofully tired from the dairy work, the pickling, the canning, etc., cannot you see that it is some compensation to know that my husband and babies will have pure cream and butter, that my pickles are not crisp because of the use of alum, that boric acid does not enter into my chicken salad and boned turkey, and that the latter are really chicken and turkey? Besides, our hobbies and dream castles lighten the monotony wonderfully. I have three friends who are quite proud of their blooded poultry. Must they be condemned as lacking in ambition and having no craving for the "higher life" simply because they "made chickens take them to St. Louis last year?"

We are perhaps overworked often and become despondent and nervous, but do not some city wives go to Palm Beach for rest and some husbands to Europe for a stomach? If it is a question of bondage, personally I would rather be a slave to the fresh, sweet soil and my babies than to a pug dog and a social rule that obliges me to leave my dress waist at home and to "do" the "high-up handshake" into the wee sma' hours. Pardon me, I do not wish to be rude. But you are independent and will credit this to my different bringing up, will you not?

As to this farmer sister of mine, her story is the most pitifully tragic thing that has come to my notice for many a day. It has been my observation that modern martyrs' crowns are usually uncomfortable and profitless, and if I knew her I should beg her to follow your plan of campaign to the letter. But you forgot to tell her to eat breakfast with her family—and my husband builds the morning fires.

Blenco, Iowa   *Mrs. F. A. Nisewanger*

You may be interested to know that I was requested to read the article, "One Farmer's Wife" in the last issue of *The Independent* to the Clinton County Farmers' Institute. Probably 250 people listened with marked interest to the reading of the paper.

No public discussion was attempted, but in many private discussions it was variously estimated from pure fiction to cold facts, and apparently awakened a good deal of thought.

De Witt, Iowa   *(Rev.) J. J. Mitchell*

My husband and I read the article on "One Farmer's Wife" in last week's *Independent.* We have taken your magazine for over 20 years. We have always loved its pages, and read it with deep respect and interest. The article spoken of was a shock to our family. I would like to send you a *sunnier* picture of a farmer's wife and her *life* in *Illinois* than that poor lady has depicted. I do not wish money for it, but I would like to have the Eastern people know of the handsome homes, the culture and higher life of farmers 30 miles west of Peoria. We live on a beautiful farm of 200 acres, worth $150 an acre; have a house in town and 160 acres in Canada. My husband and I have been members many years of the First Congregational Church of C——. I am a member of the Woman's Club in town, composed of ladies of wide culture and who have traveled in Europe. My daughter is a student at the Chicago Musical College and will graduate this year.

I was married in '76, went to the Centennial on my wedding trip, have one child, the daughter. Have never made garden or done a washing without help. Perhaps I have milked a cow two or three times in 28 years. Have kept a good girl many years and paid $2.50 a week. We take $30 worth of daily papers and magazines and weeklies. Last summer we took five dailies. We have a carriage, buggy, sleigh, fur robes, etc. Nearly all the farmers here have handsome carriage robes and *everything* comfortable.

When I was a young married woman I had all the cares and busy times that go with farm life, and kept it up for 19 years. When I could not get help we hired our washing and ironing done out of the house. Some years I made $90 worth of butter, often sold $60 worth of chickens, and that was *my money*. I bought lovely china, nearly furnished all my house handsomely with that money. When Sabbath morning came we always went to church in town; attended concerts that were good in town evenings. My husband is fond of travel, loves good music dearly, is an inveterate reader and well posted on the topics of the day. He usually spends three or four hours a day reading the magazines, besides the reading in the evening.

My husband has his carriage team of black Morgans and a Jersey cow to look after and makes his garden, the land being rented out. For twenty years there has been a good tenant house, where one or two men boarded, taking that much work out of the house. At the present time we both take life quietly, travel when we wish to, go to Chicago occasionally to enjoy the music and advantages there for a few days.

Another Illinois Farmer's Wife

As I was reading the piece entitled "The Farmer's Wife" it came to me that I could write another side of that sister's life, as I am standing in almost the same position as she is, if you think it worth printing. I was not born on a farm, but in a small English village in the south part of old England, and when I was a mere baby my parents brought me over the seas to New York State, and there my father lived on a rented farm. We lived thus for eleven years, from one place to another. It was most of the time too far for us children to go to school, so our mother taught us to read some at home. When I was twelve years old father came to Michigan to get a new home for his family. He bought a new piece of land and then came back for us, and we moved on to it the next spring.

Oh, there is so much to write in here between the lines of childhood times that we had in a new country of woods and wilderness! How happy we children were! But the work came into our lives as well, and hard every day work, too, for there was a large family of us; and the four oldest being girls, we had to take the place of boys in the work in the new home. Father felled the large trees and then we would help him split them up into logs, and then we would take the team to draw them up into large heaps to burn them to ashes. We could not sell timber as now to clear the land of it so that we could raise corn and potatoes among the stumps. We girls and mother helped do all this work. After the land was cleared of the wood there were the fences to be built around the fields. We laid the rails as father split them from the logs into fences. Then the land had to be got ready for crops to be planted, and it then had to be hoed and cared for, and there was the harvesting of all the crops and so it went from one year to another; but we did not get weary of it, for the little word of *love* was in all we did. Father didn't have any education, but he sent us to school winters. But I would not have you think that he was a selfish man thus to keep his wife and daughters at work out all day and then come into the house and there help to get work in there done for the next day. When I was sixteen we had a Sunday school and meetings started in our school house. We went every Sunday to the school and meeting. Such you see was my life as a farmer's daughter.

Now I must pass on to that of a farmer's wife. That came when I was nineteen years old. My husband was a man of no education at all, and was brought up not to go to church or Sunday school; to dance was his pleasure, and to such places he went. But he loved me, and I did not attend such places; so he gave it up for my sake. We commenced to go to church when we were married. Sometimes he did not feel like going, but I would ask him if we were not going to church, in a kind of loving way, and he would get ready to go. I believe it lies in every woman's power to lead her husband in right or wrong ways if she will go in the right way to do it. She must love and respect her husband, if she expects him to do the same for her. There is not man in his right mind who will not do anything for the loved one.

I am a great lover of reading. As my husband cannot read in the evening we would sit and I would read aloud to him, so he could get the good of it as well as I did. In this way he came to like to stay at home evenings to listen to the readings. He came to like books as well as I did, in his way, for he did not know how good it is to have education, which his parents neglected to give him. My work as a farmer's wife has been very much as the sister said hers has been, only I have eight children to bring up. They may not have the polish of some children, but I can say, if I am their mother, that they are a credit to the community they live in and I am proud of them. And do you think they would respect me if I did not respect their father? Oh, no, for a child is a close imitator of his mother in such things. I do not think my husband is selfish because he wanted me to help him out in the field and let my work in the house go till his was done. And I did not work while he ate his meals, for that was one very wrong thing for the sister to do. Why did she not sit down with him and talk to him about his work and his business? And then when she wants to make her wishes known they would know each other better and he would understand her desires better. We must keep in close touch with our loved ones, and not get the idea in our heads that we are better than they; for what is life without love in it? I have worked hard all my life, but I always find time to eat at table with my husband and children.

My oldest child is married and keeping her own home now with her little daughter. The others are at home yet, and we are a happy family. My husband has been a church member for a long time, and so are three of my children, and we go to church and Sunday school almost every Sunday. Oh, there is much to write on this theme, but it must come to a close, for I can hear some one say "She is a goody-good." But, dear sisters, I am no better than any of you are, only for God who has given this holy love through himself if we accept it for ourselves and to give to others we meet in this great world.

A Michigan Farmer's Wife

A College Professor's Wife

By the standards of the overwhelming majority of Americans in 1905, the college professor's family was wealthy. With an income of $1,100 per year, live-in help who prepared breakfast and cleaned up after dinner, and a black laundress to do the family wash, this family's life-style and quality of life far surpassed the others in this book. Yet the wife and mother felt deprived and lonely and lived almost totally in her family's world.

The workday of the college professor's wife was a long one, running from six in the morning until ten at night. After dinner she had one brief hour to herself; the rest of the time she was cook, maid, seamstress, ironer, tutor, teacher, and confidant to the family. She described in detail the chores and duties of a turn-of-the-century homemaker, mother, and wife. Like many households, hers had no running water and every drop had to be carried into the home. Aside from keeping house without the aid of the new technologies that were entering other middle-class homes—washing machines, refrigerators, vacuum cleaners—she put in a full day's work making nearly all of the family's clothes.

While she enjoyed the closeness of the family—eating noon dinners together, tutoring the youngest ones, sharing confidences with the boys—she was also lonely because the family confined her. Her relationship with her husband seemed almost business-like; their hours together were silent ones, for she sewed as he worked. In contrast, hours shared with a woman neighbor were a delight as her friend shared the time with her, reading aloud. But the college professor's wife was practically cut off from feminine sharing; her arduous tasks left her little time or energy for working or visiting with other women. Occasional nights out offered musical entertainment or lectures with other couples from the college, but she gave no indication that these activities offered her satisfying companionship.

Independent, LIX (Nov. 30, 1905), 1279-83.

Although her article revealed no sign of consciousness of her lot, the act of writing the autobiography and its publication in the *Independent* must be interpreted as a sign of her awareness of her position, for many women at the turn of the century were self-consciously examining their lives.

MANY OF the people in our town think that we members of the college faculty dwell on Mount Parnassus; that we eat of the ambrosia of books and drink of the nectar of music and painting. No burdens of ordinary mortals come near us, no sordid struggles engage us—ours is a life of high ideals and beautiful thoughts. The color and making of the next ball-gown certainly never is discussed, but in place of it there is careful planning to see if a suit and a half for the boys may be gotten out of their father's old one. The latest fad in dinner-serving is unheard of, but we professors' wives do try to learn the most attractive way to prepare the family breakfast without the luxuries of coffee and meat.

An income of $1,100 a year and four children and house rent, a taste for books, art and music, and travel—and no struggles, think you?

My day begins at six o'clock the year round with giving or superintending cold baths for the four children and myself. Then there are backs to button and hair to comb, and it is easily quarter after seven, our breakfast hour, by the time all are ready.

Bertha, a student who earns her room and board with us during term time, prepares the breakfast of oatmeal and cocoa.

After the meal there are the Professor and two boys to start off to college and school, respectively. Each needs personal inspection—a loose button tightened, an application of the whisk-broom, or the tie retouched. Then the little girls come with me into the kitchen, and we wash and put away the breakfast dishes, scalding all the milk pails and pans and skimming the cream for the butter. Then we make the beds and put upstairs in order. (Bertha cares for her own room.) The study and other living rooms come next, and when they are dusted and neat, it is time to prepare the vegetables for dinner.

It is while I am getting dinner that Ruth and Mary have their book-

lessons. We do not care to have our children enter school before the
third grade because of the class of children that attend our ward
school. The two little girls use a wooden box for a desk, sitting on two
lower ones, in a snug corner of the kitchen, where I can teach them as I
peel potatoes, pare apples or move about the room mixing a pudding.
It takes some time to prepare a meal for seven people, four of them
hungry students. One thing that makes it harder is not having any
water or sink in the house. By half after twelve the dinner is on the
table, and I have spent a morning in careful planning, with quick, sure
strokes to get all the work done, and yet have time to stop
occasionally, as I have to, to teach the children. They come first, after
all.

In winter the dinner consists of a cheap cut of meat, usually beef,
that I grind up or steam tender and then cook in all sorts of ways to
make a palatable variety; potatoes in various forms, frequently dried
beans or peas, baked or boiled, from time to time relieved by parsnips,
carrots, turnips, or maccaroni, rice and escalloped tomatoes, a large
part of the latter being bread-crumbs. For dessert, clear fruit is too
luxurious, so I prepare it with tapioca; batter pudding, corn-starch or
bread crumbs in different puddings. I begrudge the time it takes to
make these simple puddings, but we cannot afford an apple, orange or
banana apiece per diem at winter prices.

During the summer we rarely buy meat, but eat the eggs from our
own hens. We also have many fresh vegetables from our garden patch;
but we can't touch even canned ones in winter, much less dream of
fresh ones. The tomatoes used for escalloping in Winter are some I
put up from our own garden.

The dinner over, Bertha takes charge of dining-room, kitchen and
door-bell. The Professor takes care of the children, and I have one
quiet, restful hour alone, the only one in the twenty-four that I can call
all mine. That is not always uninterrupted, as every mother knows. In
that hour I have to make my simple toilet for the afternoon and take a
nap. A cat-nap it is; but oh! it is so much needed, for housework tires
me out. Perhaps if the muscles for housework had been developed in
girlhood it would not wear on me so much. Then, best of all in my
hour, I lie down on the bed and read for twenty mintues— sometimes a
full half hour. I read—I devour rather—some rare morsel of rich,

At the turn of the twentieth century, the most common women's work was unpaid labor in the home. This 1905 photograph shows a housewife drying dishes in her kitchen. Culver Pictures.

condensed thought-food, and I digest it later as I sew, enjoying it quietly, deeply.

From two-thirty until ten o'clock I sew, stopping at half-past five for a half-hour's walk with my husband and some of the children, followed by supper at six. If informal callers drop in during the afternoon, I continue sewing, they often bringing theirs with them.

I give half an hour of music to each of the children during the afternoon as I sew. Except for his half hour at the piano or violin, each child lives out of doors all afternoon, no matter what the weather, and a rosy, jolly little group they make. On my constitutional with James the children skip and dance around us as we walk out over the prairie toward the glorious West sky. Then comes the most pleasant meal of the day, supper. Then my husband's class work is over, and we are all hungry from the fresh air, and we have the fun of a foreign language. We have French and German suppers on alternate days, in conversation only, the bill of fare being good American cereals and bread and milk.

After supper, if it lacks seven o'clock, the little girls' bed time, we all gather around the piano and sing some simple songs in English, French and German, or I play while the children dance. The little dances they know I teach them on Saturday mornings, when Bertha takes some of my housework.

At seven, James carries a little girl upstairs on each shoulder and puts them to bed, a privilege he has made his own. In the meantime, I have my talk with the boys. They tell their little confidences more freely being both together, each one helping the other by loving suggestion. They are so unalike that each has great admiration for the other. In half an hour they scamper upstairs and take possession of their father.

By eight o'clock my turn comes. James sits by me as I sew, and we talk alone together for the first time in the day. Sometimes he reads aloud to me, but at half after eight his evening's study begins. If my work is on a garment that does not need turning and shifting about so that I make no motions to divert his attention from his books, I sit silently by him sewing, sewing without a word, glad to be near my faithful, plodding man. When ten o'clock comes, I bid him good-night and go off to my little Ruth and Mary, leaving him still working.

Sometimes a neighbor spends the evening with me, sewing or reading aloud. What a delight to be read to as I sew! Because I loved books and music too well, I hardly knew how to handle a needle before I was married. But the college days and study in Europe help the needle thru hard places now. All this sewing does not mean that I am an atom in a sweatshop system. I means that I am taking the only, the last way possible, to make ends meet on our salary and yet live with my children in their work and in their play. My husband's clothing and my winter under-woolens are all that we buy ready made. I make sturdy jackets for James to save the wear on his sacque coat, and keep a piece of carpet in his study chair to save the trousers. Of course, all repairs, relinings and pressing on his clothing I attend to. My coats and dresses are my hardest tasks, harder even than the boys' suits. All of the children's clothing, both outer and undergarments, I alone make, many of them from the sound parts of their parents' clothing. Then there are carpets to mend, comfortables to make, and other household supplies to keep up. The regular weekly stocking darning and other mending for an active family of six is no small item.

Our student helper, Bertha, does her own ironing and bakes the bread twice a week. I frequently help her with the mid-week baking. She cooks breakfast and supper, washes the dinner and supper dishes, and fills the lamps. On Friday afternoon and Saturday morning she gives me two extra hours each for sweeping. In exchange for these services she receives her board and room, well furnished and heated, and enters into the family life as one of us at meals and other times. Often I help her with her lessons during the evening.

One part of the week's work I hire done for me. That is the washing and as much of the ironing as can be crowded into the same day, subject to the discretion of our whimsical dusky Minerva. The rest of the ironing for the famly falls to me.

The poorly built house adds to my difficulties as maid of all work. All of the water has to be carried into the house from the cistern pump, ten or fifteen feet from the kitchen doorsteps. There is no sink or waste pipe of any kind, so all the waste water has to be carried some distance from the house and thrown on the ground. When it is below zero those two things amount to hardships, almost, for a family of our size uses a good deal of water. We have no cellar, except a small excavation in the clay soil under our dining room. It is called a cyclone cellar, and might be used as such if we were not in as great danger of drowning—as it is utterly useless for anything but frogs. When we asked our landlord to have it drained he laughed, and answered that he did not think we needed any more piping than the nightly frog songs. That is all that came of it, except, perhaps, a doctor's bill or two, but other interesting features about the house have their part in these little notes, "For services rendered." Rain and snow and wind sift in around the door and window frames and thru the corners of the house, where we can often see light shining at the joint in the mopboard. Certainly they swell the fuel bill. The care of four stoves, three of them heating and one a cook stove, is no small matter. The boys help their father carry the coal from the barn, the only place to store it. Soft coal is bulky and dirty, but anthracite is far beyond our means here in the Middle West. The same strong arms bring in much of the water also.

We pay eighteen dollars ($18) a month for this poorly built, eight small-roomed house, its three lots and barn made of piano boxes and other odds and ends of lumber. We could not hope to rent a better built house, merely a larger one, for more money unless we were willing to go over forty dollars. Families have come to live in our town faster than houses could be properly built, and it is hard on the man who has not capital enough to build for himself. The three lots that go with our leaky house are very useful, for they furnish us a garden of rich soil in Summer and a playground for children and chickens in Winter. The cow and the coal repose in our barn, and each has about equal space in its luxurious proportions. That cow is a big saving of money, but it adds to our labor, for we make our own butter, but we must have it to help those proverbial "ends." There is plenty of prairie south and east of us for pasturage.

Others of the faculty are trying to tie those flying *ends* too. Mrs. A—— does about what I do for her three little girls and gives piano lessons to the neighborhood besides. Mrs. B—— has her three year old boy and housework, including the washing, and tutors in mathematics and Latin five hours every day, four of the five hours coming after seven o'clock at night, when the little fellow is in bed. Mrs. C——, who has no children, writes book reviews and has charge of the Women's and Children's Page in our paper. All of the wives of the faculty are busy

women, trying each in her own way to add to her husband's pittance.
Where the men are not full professors, that pittance is less than my
husband's.

With all this straining to live comes a wish from the President and
Trustees of the college that we mingle more in town society; that it will
be good advertisement for the college to be well represented everywhere. Who can afford the evening dress to go? Or the evening's
sewing left undone? Who can return invitations? Who has the
strength—and this is at the highest premium—who has the strength to
spare? Not one of the wives of the Trustees who desire this has ever
called on a professor's wife, much less done anything to bring the
college people into her circle of acquaintances. We meet them at the
college receptions; they always express their interest in the college,
and that is all.

The little social life we have is among ourselves almost entirely. We
gather informally at a house for a hour and a half or so, chat awhile,
then, perhaps have an impromptu entertainment of music, or an
account of a book lately read, a bit of a lecture on a topic of general
academic interest; then light refreshments and home by ten o'clock, for the next
day's hard work is before us all. There are college lectures, debates
and entertainments that those of us who have few or no children
attend; but the children mean spending no admission fees, however
small. Of course, it would be a real benefit to the students as well as
ourselves if we could keep in touch with these broadening influences;
but it is in other ways we are forced to help them. It is expected that we
subscribe to the football, baseball, glee club, Y. M. and Y. W. C. A.,
and other college student funds. To some of these we would volunteer
to add as liberally as we could, but not to all, when we hardly are
clothed warmly enough all Winter. Anyway, we do not like to have the
sum we are expected to raise announced to us, with the request that we
see that the vote passes in faculty-meeting. If the request, or demand
rather, came from the student-body it could be resisted.

There is one way in which James and I rejoice to help the students.
Whenever we treat ourselves to a roast of meat we share it with one or
two self-supporting students. It is reward enough that they bring us
their joy or suffering, even coming back after graduation to share their
life-crises with us.

enervate = deprive of strength, nerve

It has been suggested to us not to live in such and such a house because it is not in keeping with the dignity of our position (!). We are to entertain in such and such a way, for we have had the best advantages in social life that this country can boast (!). (I add the exclamation with respect to our superiors.) The discrepancy comes between the ideal and the actual possibilities of our salaries. We who have had comforts, even luxuries, do not avoid them now because we were satiate. True, our tastes and education make us companions of the refined in easy circumstances, but our incomes are those of mechanics. The mechanic may be refined and have lofty ambitions, but he does not *need* travel, close contact with good libraries and large minds, an intimacy with the fine arts and the sciences to keep him ready to help those under him, as a professor does. It is enervating to work by one's self, going over the same ground every year, always alone, with but a new book or two on the subject. Oh! how I long that my husband may have the chance to study under somebody, with some one of his own or greater education and intelligence! If it were but for a Summer it would give him a new impetus. But how is this possible on our $1,100 a year? This is just how it all goes:

pulse

Rent	$216.00
Food (including fodder for cow in winter)	300.00
Clothing	125.00
Fuel and light	55.00
Hired help for washing (52 weeks at $1.25)	65.00
Hired help for housecleaning (4 days at $1.25)	5.00
Magazines and books (including technical books for professor and school books for children)	35.00
Church and college contributions	40.00
Life insurance and fire insurance on furniture	105.00
Doctor's and dentist's bills	20.00
Carfare, postage, etc.	30.00
Household furnishings, tinware, garden implements, etc,	40.00
Sundries (Christmas presents and other expenses larger than average)	64.00

Where does the possibility to travel and study elsewhere come in here? To get away from one's cow and vegetable patch must help to *keen perception*

came to appear meritorious

quicken a man's wits in itself, to say nothing of our stultifying Summer heat.

It is because we with our needs and tastes are not receiving a living salary that there is a constantly changing element in the faculty, especially among young married men with no children. They consider their connection with our college temporary, taking it as a stepping-stone to larger institutions. They do us a real harm with their inexperience in teaching and their restlessness. An occasional one would not be so detrimental, but it is demoralizing for the students to change instructors in a study every few years, just as the former one begins to understand how to teach it. This spirit of self-interest is more noticeable in the science and music departments than others, it seems to me.

I overheard a conversation between James and Mr. E——, a Ph.D. from Halle, a while ago. They were standing in our little hallway when Mr. E—— asked James for a letter of recommendation to a teachers' agency.

"Why do you want one?" James asked.

"Stay here! I'd rust."

"Oh, no, you wouldn't. Men who carry double schedules don't rust."

"Perhaps you can stand grinding all your life for nothing, but I've got to have a better place."

I thought about it afterward. "A better place!" He might find a more remunerative one, but after all, is there a better place than here and time than now, for giving one's best? Are not these hardworking, serious young men and women worth helping as much as their more delicate, high-strung Eastern cousins?

"Shall the Professor 'Stay Put,'"
by Another College Professor's Wife

"Another College Professor's Wife" responded to the original article, and agreed that the life of a college professor was difficult and unrewarding. In detailing the arduous life, the second woman dealt almost entirely with the professor's life; her own plight is ignored, except insofar as it was defined by her husband's work and world. This reinforces the sense at the time that few married woman had lives independently defined from those of their husbands.

IN A LATE number of *The Independent,* "A College Professor's Wife" tells a story the truth of whose details must have touched a responsive chord in the breasts of many of her sisters. Her picture has the merit of a good sermon; each of us is sure that she "meant me." But with her conclusion that the ideal professor ought philosophically to accept the uncomfortable conditions which she describes, the present writer does not find herself in accord.

Out west of the Mississippi River and not far from the Missouri is a little college town whose "university" is the center of the community life. Surrounding the town on all sides are ranches and farms; beyond these lie the prairies stretching to the unbroken circle of the horizon. In the town itself conditions are not unlike those in which "A College Professor's Wife" lives.

Here the professors carry a "double schedule." The salaries are small; expenses in general correpspond to those given by "A College Professor's Wife." We are almost all of us "hewers of wood and drawers of water." In winter the husband cares for the fires, splits the wood, clears off the snow, in order that money may be saved to pay the insurance premiums which fall due in the summer. In the summer we care for our gardens, adopt a vegetarian diet and forego a summer migration in order that the money may be saved for the fuel bill which falls due in early winter. Like the Puritans, who planted corn in summer that they might have food for the winter, and dug clams in summer to save using the fresh corn, we work during the summer that we may live during the winter, and work during the winter that we may live thru the summer. And so we exist from year to year.

Here, too, we faculty folk are expected to contribute to student organizations, to entertain classes, clubs and individuals. The occasional semi-distinguished guest is quartered upon the professor whose subject is most nearly related to the stranger's specialty. The lecturer on radium dines with the professor of physics—and the *Frau Professorin* cooks the modest roast; the writer of verse or fiction goes to the house of the professor of English. The baccalaureate speaker and commencement orator are honored above the common run by being entertained by the president—and Madame President bakes the cake.

But in our ranks of overcrowded, poorly paid professors, they do not keep off the rust. In nine out of ten cases the same courses of study are offered unchanged year after year, for the simple reason that lack of time and meagerness of resources prevent anything else. Our faculty men seldom come in contact with better trained minds than their own, for there is no money for travel and we are in far Cathay. Even in the rare instances when a man has managed to save enough money for a year of study at one of the larger universities, his departure is not looked upon with favor, and leave of absence is not infrequently refused. The attitude of the trustees seems to be: "If you know enough to teach your present subjects, you don't need leave of absence for study. If you do need further study, then you don't know enough to teach and we'd better get some one else." One can understand that to a new man coming in from a college where self development, scholarship and orginality are the basis of work, this situation seems odd. Yet it is common enough in the smaller colleges west of the Mississippi. Is it surprising that the professors who remain long have somewhat lax ideals of scholarship, that their views are narrow, that ultimately the intellecutal standards and opinions, the educational methods of the incoming younger men seem to them incompatible with the needs of the community? Is is surprising that the younger men pass on?

Another College Professor's Wife

Maybe they need jobs?
become - selfish. (self centered)

The Question of Labor and Capital

From Lithuania to the Chicago Stockyards—An Autobiography: Antanas Kaztauskis

In 1904, two young journalists and aspiring novelists arrived in Chicago. Both in their mid-20s, and both pro-organized labor, Ernest Poole and Upton Sinclair had come to the city to witness firsthand the protracted and violent stockyards strike of that year. Poole got there first and, along with serving as the press agent for the workers' union (the Amalgamated Meat Cutters and Butcher Workmen, or AMCBW), he prepared articles for the *Independent, Outlook,* and *World Today* magazines.

One of the strike articles in particular illuminated the human dimensions not only of this bloody labor conflict, but also of the adjustments and adaptations that a non-English-speaking peasant from eastern Europe had to make to survive in his new urban world of Chicago and the stockyards. Antanas Kaztauskis, a Lithuanian immigrant, had escaped his homeland, and the prospect of conscription into the Russian army, by secretly buying his ticket to America and bribing the Russian soldiers who guarded the borders. While Kaztauskis's exit was treacherous and at times uncertain, he knew his destination: Chicago, with jobs available in the stockyards, a handful of acquaintances from home already living and working there, and a self-conscious Lithuanian-American community with its own newspaper, church, grammar school, and benevolent and musical societies.

In October 1904, two months after the *Independent* had published "From Lithuania to the Chicago Stockyards," the second of the two journalists arrived in the city. Appearing one day at the union's headquarters, he announced both himself and his reason for being there. "Hello! I'm Upton Sinclair!" stated the smiling young man in the wide-brimmed hat. "And I've come here to write the Uncle Tom's Cabin of the Labor Movement!"[1] A year and a half later his novel,

Independent, LVII (Aug. 4, 1904), 241-48.
    1. Ernest Poole, *The Bridge: My Own Story* (New York, 1940), 95.

The Jungle, both shocked and outraged millions of Americans. The novel's impact was far different from what Sinclair had intended, for *The Jungle* did not precipitate a massive outpouring of support for either the labor movement or democratic socialism. Instead, it focused public sensitivity, even horror, on the filth and slime in the meatpacking industry, and one of its results was the enactment of the Pure Food and Drug Act of 1906. Sinclair had been unpersuasive as a political propagandist, and he admitted later that, as a muckraking writer, "I aimed at the public's heart, and by accident I hit it in the stomach."[2]

Both Antanas Kaztauskis and Jurgis Rudkis, Sinclair's hero in *The Jungle,* were Lithuanians, and both anguished over and tried to resolve the tensions between their traditional ways and the harsh demands and realities of "Packingtown." Having worked and lived as part of an extended family, Kaztauskis had expected to marry his sweetheart Alexandria and, as newlyweds, to "come back to my father's house and live with him." He had ventured to Chicago, however, where family and kinship ties could not survive in the same unquestioned way they had on his father's isolated farm.

In Chicago the pace of life was considerably faster. "Be quick, damn you, be quick"—these were the words he heard as he queued up outside the stockyards each morning with hundreds, even thousands, of other immigrants, each hopeful that he would be selected for that day's employment. And these were the words he heard as, uncounted times a day at work, he performed the same monotonous task, a victim of the speed-up, the minutely specialized division of labor, and the conveyor belt, which inexorably, and at precisely the same rapid interval, brought him a dead hog or steer to slice, saw, or hack apart.

Along with thousands of other workers, Kaztauskis and Rudkis had the same remedy for survial in Packingtown: organization of a labor union. And it was in the summer of 1904, in an upsurge of labor solidarity, that twenty-three thousand packinghouse workers and seven thousand sympathetic mechanical tradesmen struck against their bosses for a minimum wage of twenty cents a hour. "You must get money to live well," Kaztauskis explained, "and to get money you must combine. I cannot bargain alone with the Meat Trust."

Allying themselves with unskilled workers like Kaztauskis were the skilled workers, the butchers, who knew that unless a minimum wage

2. Upton Sinclair, *The Jungle* (repr.: Cambridge, Mass., 1972), viii.

were won for the unskilled, cutthroat job competition would drive all wages down. Technology, the division of labor, the speed-up, and the vast pool of immigrant and other cheap labor—these developments had wedded the economic interests of the skilled and unskilled in the stockyards. The "facts are these," a leader of the butchers' union explained. "Twenty years ago the trade of the butchers was one of the best in the country." Then, after the consolidation of smaller packinghouses into a handful of "large packing houses . . . they began a system to crowd out the expert butchers and replace them by cheaper men in every way. . . ." The owners "divided the business up into gangs consisting of enough to dress the bullock, one man doing only one thing . . . which makes it possible for the proprietor to take a man in off from the street . . . and today the expert workers are in many cases crowded out and cheap Polackers and Hungarians put in their places. . . ." Worse yet for the butchers, "if the packers refuse to agree to any minimum wage for the unskilled, how long will it be before they attempt to reduce the wages of the skilled men?"[3] Rather than take that risk, the butchers decided to take up arms with their unskilled allies.

The strike, however, was hopeless from the beginning. The nation was in a depression, unemployment was rampant, and, caught up in their own economic woes, as many as five thousand people lined up outside the stockyards each morning to replace the strikers. After ten weeks, the strikers, sullen and beaten, drifted back to work. But the villains who emerged from this defeat were not merely the packing-house owners and managers, but also the black strikebreakers, several thousand of whom had been transported into the stockyards in the same railroad cars that would later carry out the products of their labor. One observer estimated that eighteen thousand blacks served as strikebreakers, with almost fourteen hundred arriving in one trainload. Although these figures were probably exaggerated, to the strikers black "scabs" seemed to be everywhere. And, at times, the strikers' animosities boiled over. A settlement-house worker in the stockyards witnessed a mob of women and children chasing a black man down the street, crying: "Kill the fink, kill the fink." Black people were hauled off streetcars; blacks innocently walking the city's streets

3. Homer D. Call, Syracuse, N.Y., to Frank Morrison, Washington, D.C., Feb. 20, 1899, American Federation of Labor Papers, State Historical Society of Wisconsin, Madison.

were knifed, kicked, and beaten, while still others were struck with rocks and other missiles.[4]

Antanas Kaztauskis, Jurgis Rudkis, and other members of the stockyards union had had their aspirations for first-class economic and democratic citizenship crushed during the 1904 strike. Not for another dozen years—not until World War I—would the workers in Packingtown organize another union. Moreover, the words "black" and "scab" were now synonymous in the minds of many whites in the stockyards. "It was the niggers that whipped you in line," South Carolina's Senator Ben Tillman told a group of whites in the stockyards after the defeat. "They were the club with which your brains were beaten out."[5] It was not mere words, however, but another strike, the bloody teamsters' strike of 1905 (see the next autobiography, "The Chicago Strike: A Teamster"), that made more indelible the image of blacks as a "scab race." ∧ incap of being deleted or obliterated

THIS IS NOT my real name, because if this story is printed it may be read back in Lithuania, and I do not want to get my father and the ugly shoemaker into trouble with the Russian Government.

It was the shoemaker who made me want to come to America. He was a traveling shoemaker, for on our farms we tan our own cowhides, and the shoemaker came to make them into boots for us. By traveling he learned all the news and he smuggled in newspapers across the frontier from Germany. We were always glad to hear him talk.

I can never forget that evening four years ago. It was a cold December. We were in a big room in our log house in Lithuania. My good, kind, thin old mother sat near the wide fireplace, working her brown spinning wheel, with which she made cloth for our shirts and coats and pants. I sat on the floor in front of her with my knee-boots off and my feet stretched out to the fire. My feet were cold, for I had been out with my young brother in the freezing sheds milking the cows and feeding the sheep and geese. I leaned my head on her dress and kept yawning and thinking about my big goose feather bed. My father sat and smoked his pipe across the fireplace. Between was a kerosene

4. William M. Tuttle, Jr., "Labor Conflict and Racial Violence: The Black Worker in Chicago, 1894-1919," *Labor History,* X (Summer 1969), 413-14.

5. *Ibid.,* 415.

lamp on a table, and under it sat the ugly shoemaker on a stool finishing a big yellow boot. His sleeves were rolled up; his arms were thin and bony, but you could see how strong the fingers and wrist were, for when he grabbed the needle he jerked it through and the whole arm's length up. This arm kept going up and down. Every time it went up he jerked back his long mixed-up red hair and grunted. And you could just see his face—bony and shut together tight, and his narrow sharp eyes looking down. Then his head would go down again, and his hair would get all mixed up. I kept watching him. My fat, older brother, who sat behind with his fat wife, grinned and said: "Look out or your eyes will make holes in the leather." My brother's eyes were always dull and sleepy. Men like him stay in Lithuania.

At last the boot was finished. The little shoemaker held it up and looked at it. My father stopped smoking and looked at it. "That's a good boot," said my father. The shoemaker grunted. "That's a damn poor boot," he replied (instead of "damn" he said "skatina"), "a rough boot like all your boots, and so when you grow old you are lame. *[crippled]* You have only poor things, for rich Russians get your good things, and yet you will not kick up against them. Bah!"

"I don't like your talk," said my father, and he spit into the fire, as he always did when he began to think. "I am honest. I work hard. We get along. That's all. So what good will such talk do me?"

"You!" cried the shoemaker, and he now threw the boot on the floor so that our big dog lifted up his head and looked around. "It's not you at all. It's the boy—that boy there!" and he pointed to me. "That boy must go to America!"

Now I quickly stopped yawning and I looked at him all the time after this. My mother looked frightened and she put her hand on my head. "No, no; he is only a boy," she said. "Bah!" cried the shoemaker, pushing back his hair, and then I felt he was looking right through me. "He is eighteen and a man. You know where he must go in three years more." We all knew he meant my five years in the army. "Where is your oldest son? Dead. Oh, I know the Russians—the man-wolves! I served my term, I know how it is. Your son served in Turkey in the mountains. Why not here? Because they want foreign soldiers here to beat us. He had four roubles ($2.08) pay for three months, and with that he had to pay men like me to make his shoes and clothes. Oh, the wolves! They let him soak in rain, standing guard all night in the snow and ice he froze, the food was God's food, the vodka was cheap and rotten! Then he died. The wolves—the man-wolves! Look at this book." He jerked a Roman Catholic prayer book from his bag on the floor. "Where would I go if they found this on me? Where is Wilhelm Birbell?"

At this my father spit hard again into the fire and puffed his pipe fast.

"Where is Wilhelm Birbell," cried the shoemaker, and we all kept quiet. We all knew. Birbell was a rich farmer who smuggled in prayer books from Germany so that we all could pray as we liked, instead of the Russian Church way. He was caught one night and they kept him two years in the St. Petersburg jail, in a cell so narrow and short that he could not stretch out his legs, for they were very long. This made him lame for life. Then they sent him to Irkutsk, down in Siberia. There he sawed logs to get food. He escaped and now he is here in Chicago. But at that time he was in jail.

"Where is Wilhelm Birbell?" cried the shoemaker. "Oh, the wolves! And what is this?" He pulled out an old American newspaper, printed in the Lithuanian language, and I remember he tore it he was so angry. "The world's good news is all kept away. We can only read what Russian officials print in their papers. Read? No, you can't read or write your own language, because there is no Lithuanian school— only the Russian school—you can only read and write Russian. Can you? No, you can't! Because even those Russian schools make you pay to learn, and you have no money to pay. Will you never be ashamed—all you? Listen to me."

Now I looked at my mother and her face looked frightened, but the shoemaker cried still louder. "Why can't you have your own Lithuanian school? Because you are like dogs—you have nothing to say—you have no town meetings or province meetings, no elections. You are slaves! And why can't you even pay to go to their Russian school? Because they get all your money. Only twelve acres you own, but you pay eighty roubles ($40) taxes. You must work twelve days on your Russian roads. Your kind old wife must plow behind the oxen, for I saw her last summer, and she looked tired. You must all slave, but still your rye and wheat brings little money, because they cheat you bad. Oh, the wolves—how fat they are! And so your boy must never read or write, or think like a man should think."

But now my mother cried out, and her voice was shaking. "Leave us alone—you leave us! We need no money—we trade our things for the things we need at the store—we have all we need—leave us alone!"

Then my fat brother grinned and said to the shoemaker, "You always stir up young men to go to America. Why don't you go yourself?"

I remember that the little shoemaker had pulled a big crooked pipe out of his bag. Now he took a splinter from the basket of splinters which hung on the wall and he lit his pipe and puffed it. His face showed me that he felt bad. "I am too old," he said, "to learn a new trade. These boots are no good in America. America is not place for us old rascals. My son is in Chicago in the stockyards, and he writes to me. They have hard knocks. If you are sick or old there and have no money you must die. That Chicago place has trouble, too. Do you see that light? That is kerosene. Do you remember the price went up last year? That is Rockefeller. My son writes me about him. He is another man-wolf. A few men like him are grabbing all the good things,—the oil and coal and meat and everything. But against these men you can strike if you are young. You can read free papers and prayer books. In Chicago there are prayer books for every man and woman. You can have free meetings and talk out what you think. And so if you are young you can change all these troubles. But I am old. I can feel it now, this winter. So I only tell young men to go." He looked hard at me and I looked at him. He kept talking. "I tell them to go where they can choose their own kind of God—where they can learn to read and write, and talk, and think like men—and have good things!"

He kept looking at me, but he opened the newspaper and held it up. "Some day," he said, "I will be caught and sent to jail, but I don't care. I got this from my son, who reads all he can find at night. It had to be smuggled in. I lend it many times to many young men. My son got it from the night school and he put it in Lithuanian for me to see." Then he bent over the paper a long time and his lips moved. At last he looked into the fire and fixed his hair, and then his voice was shaking and very low: " 'We know these are true things—that all men are born free and equal—that God gives them rights which no man can take away—that among these rights are life, liberty and the getting of happiness.' "

He stopped, I remember, and looked at me, and I was not breathing. He said it again. " 'Life, liberty and the getting of happiness.' Oh, that is what you want."

My mother began to cry. "He cannot go if his father commands him to stay," she kept saying. I knew this was true, for in Lithuania a father can command his son till he dies.

"No, he must not go," said the shoemaker, "if his father commands him to stay." He turned and looked hard at my father. My father was looking into the fire. "If he goes," said my father, "those Russians will never let him come back." My mother cried harder. We all waited for him to say something else. In about five minutes the shoemaker got up and asked, "Well, what do you say,—the army or America?" But my father shook his head and would not say anything. Soon my brother began yawning and took his fat wife and went to bed. The little shoemaker gathered his tools into his big bag and threw it over his shoulder. His shoulder was crooked. Then he came close to me and looked at me hard.

"I am old," he said, "I wish I was young. And you must be old soon and that will be too late. The army—the man-wolves! Bah! it is terrible."

After he was gone my father and I kept looking at the fire. My mother stopped crying and went out. Our house was in two parts of two rooms each. Between the parts was an open shed and in this shed was a big oven, where she was baking bread that night. I could hear her pull it out to look at it and then push it back. Then she came in and sat down beside me and began spinning again. I leaned against her dress and watched the fire and thought about America. Sometimes I looked at my father, and she kept looking at him, too, but he would not say anything. At last my old mother stopped spinning and put her hand on my forehead.

"Alexandria is a fine girl," she whispered. This gave me a quick bad feeling. Alexandria was the girl I wanted to marry. She lived about ten miles away. Her father liked my father and they seemed to be glad that I loved her. I had often been thinking at night how in a few years I would go with my uncle to her house and ask her father and mother to give her to me. I could see the wedding all ahead—how we would go to her house on Saturday night and they would have music there and many people and we would have a sociable time. Then in the morning we would go to the church and be married and come back to my father's house and live with him. I saw it all ahead, and I was sure we would be very happy. Now I began thinking of this. I could see her fine soft eyes and I hated to go away. My old mother kept her hands moving on my forehead. "Yes, she is a nice girl; a kind, beautiful girl," she kept whispering. We sat there till the lamp went out. Then the fire got low and the room was cold and we went to bed. But I could not sleep and kept thinking.

The next day my father told me that I could not go until the time came for the army, three years ahead. "Stay until then and then we will see," he said. My mother was very glad and so was I, because of Alexandria. But in the coldest part of that winter my dear old mother got sick and died. The neighbors all came in and sang holy songs for two days and nights. The priest was there and my father bought fine candles. Two of the neighbors made a coffin. At last it was all over. For a long a time our log house was always quiet.

That summer the shoemaker came again and talked with me. This time I was very eager to go to America, and my father told me I could go.

One morning I walked over to say good-by to Alexandria. It was ten miles and the road was dusty, so I carried my boots over my shoulder, as we always did, and I put them on when I came near her house. When I saw her I felt very bad, and so did she. I had the strongest wish I ever had to take hold of her and keep her all my life. We stayed together till it was dark and night fogs came up out of the field grass, and we could hardly see the house. Then she said good-by. For many nights I kept remembering the way she looked up at me.

The next night after supper I started. It is against the law to sell tickets to America, but my father saw the secret agent in the village and he got a ticket from Germany and found us a guide. I had bread and cheese and honey and vodka and clothes in my bag. Some of the neighbors walked a few miles and said good-by and then went back. My father and my younger brother walked on all night with the guide and me. At daylight we came to the house of a man the guide knew.

We slept there and that night I left my father and young brother. My father gave me $50 besides my ticket. The next morning before light we were going through the woods and we came to the frontier. Three roads run along the frontier. On the first road there is a soldier every mile, who stands there all night. On the second road is a soldier every half mile, and on the third road is a soldier every quarter of a mile. The guide went ahead through the woods. I hid with my big bag behind a bush and whenever he raised his hand I sneaked along. I felt cold all over and sometimes hot. He told me that sometimes he took twenty immigrants together, all without passports, and then he could not pass the soldiers and so he paid a soldier he knew one dollar a head to let them by. He said the soldier was very strict and counted them to see that he was not being cheated.

So I was in Germany. Two days after that we reached Tilzit and the guide took me to the railroad man. This man had a crowd of immigrants in a room, and we started that night on the railroad— fourth class. It was bad riding sometimes. I used to think of Alexandria. We were all green and slow. The railroad man used to say to me, "You will have to be quicker than this in Chicago," and he was right. We were very slow in the stations where we changed trains, and he used to shout at us then, and one old German man who spoke Lithuanian told me what the man was calling us. When he told me this I hurried, and so did the others, and we began to learn to be quicker. It took three days to get to Hamburg. There we were put in a big house called a barracks, and we waited a week. The old German man told me that the barracks men were cheating us. He had been once to Cincinnati in America to visit his son, who kept a saloon. His old, long pipe was stolen there. He kept saying, "Dem grafters, dem grafters," in a low voice whenever they brought food to sell, for our bags were now empty. They kept us there till our money was half spent on food. I asked the old man what kind of American men were grafters, and he said "All kinds in Cincinnati, but more in Chicago!" I knew I was going to Chicago, and I began to think quicker. I thought quicker yet on the boat. I saw men playing cards. I played and lost $1.86 in my new money, till the old man came behind me and said, "Dem grafters." When I heard this I got scared and threw down my cards. That old man used to point up at the rich people looking down at us and say "Dem grafters." They were the richest people I had ever seen—the boat was the biggest boat I had ever seen—the machine that made it go was very big, and so was the horn that blew in a fog. I felt everything get bigger and go quicker every day.

It was the most when we came to New York. We were driven in a thick crowd to the railroad station. The old man kept pointing and saying "Grafters, grafters," till the guide punched him and said, "Be quick, damn you, be quick." ... "I will be quick pretty soon," said the old man to me, "and den I will get back dot pipe in Cincinnati. And when I will be quicker still, alreddy, I will steal some odder man's pipe. Every quick American man is a grafter." I began to believe that this was true, but I was mixed up and could not think long at one time. Everything got quicker—worse and worse—till then at last I was in a boarding house by the stockyards in Chicago, with three Lithuanians, who knew my father's sisters at home.

That first night we sat around in the house and they asked me, "Well, why did you come?" I told them about that first night and what the ugly shoemaker said about "life, liberty and the getting of happiness." They all leaned back and laughed. "What you need is money," they said. "It was all right at home. You wanted nothing. You ate your own meat and your own things on the farm. You made your own clothes and had your own leather. The other things you got at the Jew man's store and paid him with sacks of rye. But here you want a hundred things. Whenever you walk out you see new things you want, and you must have money to buy everything."

Then one man asked me, "How much have you?" and I told him $30. "You must buy clothes to look rich, even if you are not rich," he said. "With good clothes you will have friends."

The next morning three of these men took me to a store near the stockyards to buy a coat and pants. "Look out," said one of them. "Is he a grafter?" I asked. They all laughed. "You stand still. That is all you have to do," they said. So the Jew man kept putting on coats and I moved my arms and back and sides when they told me. We stayed there till it was time for dinner. Then we bought a suit. I paid $5 and then I was to pay $1 a week for five weeks.

In the afternoon I went to a big store. There was a man named Elias. "He is not a grafter," said my friends. He was nice to me and gave me

implicate of grafter = every one is grafter

good advice how to get a job. I bought two shirts, a hat, a collar, a necktie, two pairs of socks and some shoes. We kept going upstairs and downstairs. I saw one Lithuanian man buying everything for his wife and three children, who would come here the next week from Lithuania. My things cost me $8. I put these on right away and then I began to feel better.

The next night they took me for a walk down town. We would not pay to ride, so we walked so long that I wanted to take my shoes off, but I did not tell them this. When we came there I forgot my feet. We stood by one theater and watched for half an hour. Then we walked all around a store that filled one whole block and had walls of glass. Then we had a drink of whisky, and this is better than vodka. We felt happier and looked into *cafés.* We saw shiny carriages and automobiles. I saw men with dress suits, I saw women with such clothes that I could not think at all. Then my friends punched me and I turned around and saw one of these women, and with her was a gentlman in a fine dress suit. I began looking harder. It was the Jew man that sold me my suit. "He is a grafter," said my friends. "See what money can do." Then we walked home and I felt poor and my shoes got very bad.

That night I felt worse. We were tired out when we reached the stockyards, so we stopped on the bridge and looked into the river out there. It was so full of grease and dirt and sticks and boxes that it looked like a big, wide, dirty street, except in some places, where it boiled up. It made me sick to look at it. When I looked away I could see on one side some big fields full of holes, and these were the city dumps. On the other side were the stockyards, with twenty tall slaughter house chimneys. The wind blew a big smell from them to us. Then we walked on between the yards and the dumps and all the houses looked bad and poor. In our house my room was in the basement. I lay down on the floor with three other men and the air was rotten. I did not go to sleep for a long time. I knew then that money was everything I needed. My money was almost gone and I thought that I would soon die unless I got a job, for this was not like home. Here money was everything and a man without money must die.

The next morning my friends woke me up at five o'clock and said, "Now, if you want life, liberty and happiness," they laughed, "you must push for yourself. You must get a job. Come with us." And we went to the yards. Men and women were walking in by thousands as far as we could see. We went to the doors of one big slaughter house. There was a crowd of about 200 men waiting there for a job. They looked hungry and kept watching the door. At last a special policeman came out and began pointing to men, one by one. Each one jumped forward. Twenty-three were taken. Then they all went inside, and all the others turned their faces away and looked tired. I remember one boy sat down and cried, just next to me, on a pile of boards. Some policemen waved their clubs and we all walked on. I found some Lithuanians to talk with, who told me they had come every morning for three weeks. Soon we met other crowds coming away from other slaughter houses, and we all walked around and felt bad and tired and hungry.

That night I told my friends that I would not do this many days, but would go some place else. "Where?" they asked me, and I began to see then that I was in bad trouble, because I spoke no English. Then one man told me to give him $5 to give the special policeman. I did this and the next morning the policeman pointed me out, so I had a job. I have heard some big talk since then about my American freedom of contract, but I do not think I had much freedom in bargaining for this job with the Meat Trust. My job was in the cattle killing room. I pushed the blood along the gutter. Some people think these jobs make men bad. I do not think so. The men who do the killing are not as bad as the ladies with fine clothes who come every day to look at it, because they have to do it. The cattle do not suffer. They are knocked senseless with a big hammer and are dead before they wake up. This is done not to spare them pain, but because if they got hot and sweating with fear and pain the meat would not be so good. I soon saw that every job in the room was done like this—so as to save everything and make money. One Lithuanian, who worked with me, said, "They get all the blood out of those cattle and all the work out of us men." This was true, for we worked that first day from six in the morning till seven at night. The next day we worked from six in the morning till eight at night. The next day we had no work. So we had no good, regular hours. It was hot in the room that summer, and the hot blood made it worse.

I held this job six weeks and then I was turned off. I think some other man had paid for my job, or perhaps I was too slow. The foreman in that room wanted quick men to make the work rush, because he was paid more if the work was done cheaper and quicker. I saw now that every man was helping himself, always trying to get all the money he could. At that time I believed that all men in Chicago were grafters when they had to be. They only wanted to push themselves. Now, when I was idle I began to look about, and everywhere I saw sharp men beating out slow men like me. Even if we worked hard it did us no good. I had saved $13—$5 a week for six weeks makes $30, and take off $15 for six weeks' board and lodging and $2 for other things. I showed this to a Lithuanian, who had been here two years, and he laughed. "It will be taken from you," he said. He had saved a hundred dollars once and had begun to buy a house on the instalment plan, but something had happened that he did not know about and his landlord put him out and kept the hundred dollars. I found that many Lithuanians had been beaten this way. At home we never made a man sign contract papers. We only had him make the sign of a cross and promise he would do what he said. But this was no good in Chicago. So these sharp men were beating us.

I saw this, too, in the newspaper. I was beginning to learn English, and at night in the boarding house the men who did not play cards used to read the paper to us. The biggest word was "Graft" in red letters on the front page. Another word was "Trust." This paper kept putting these two words together. Then I began to see how every American man was trying to get money for himself. I wondered if the old German man in Cincinnati had found his pipe yet. I felt very bad and sorrowful in that month. I kept walking around wih many other Lithuanians who had no job. Our money was going and we could find nothing to do. At night we got homesick for our fine green mountains. We read all the news about home in our Lithuanian Chicago newspaper, *The Katalikas.* It is a good paper and gives all the news. In the same office we bought this song, which was written in Brooklyn by P. Brandukas. He, too, was homesick. It is sung all over Chicago now and you can hear it in the summer evenings through the open windows. In English it is something like this:

Oh, Lithuania, so dear to me,
Good-by to you, my Fatherland.

Sorrowful in my heart I leave you,
I know not who will stay to guard you.

Is it enough for me to live and enjoy between my neighbors,
In the woods with the flowers and birds?
Is it enough for me to live peaceful between my friends?
No, I must go away from my old father and mother.

The sun shines bright,
The flowers smell sweet,
The birds are singing,
They make the country glad;
But I cannot sing because I must leave you.

Those were bad days and nights. At last I had a chance to help
myself. Summer was over and Election Day was coming. The
Republican boss in our district, Jonidas, was a saloonkeeper. A friend
took me there. Jonidas shook hands and treated me fine. He taught me
to sign my name, and the next week I went with him to an office and
signed some paper, and then I could vote. I voted as I was told, and
then they got me back into the yards to work, because one big
politician owns stock in one of those houses. Then I felt that I was
getting in beside the game. I was in a combine like other sharp men.
Even when work was slack I was all right, because they got me a job in
the street cleaning department. I felt proud, and I went to the back
room in Jonidas's saloon and got him to write a letter to Alexandria to
tell her she must come soon and be my wife.

But this was just the trouble. All of us were telling our friends to
come soon. Soon they came—even thousands. The employers in the
yard liked this, because those sharp foremen are inventing new
machines and the work is easier to learn, and so these slow
Lithuanians and even green girls can learn to do it, and then the
Americans and Germans and Irish are put out and the employer saves
money, because the Lithuanians work cheaper. This was why the
American labor unions began to organize us all just the same as they
had organized the Bohemians and Poles before us.

Well, we were glad to be organized. We had learned that in Chicago
every man must push himself always, and Jonidas had taught us how
much better we could push ourselves by getting into a combine. Now,
we saw that this union was the best combine for us, because it was the

only combine that could say, "It is our business to raise your wages."

But that Jonidas—he spoilt our first union. He was sharp. First he got us to hire the room over his saloon. He used to come in at our meetings and sit in the back seat and grin. There was an Irishman there from the union headquarters, and he was trying to teach us to run ourselves. He talked to a Lithuanian, and the Lithuanian said it to us, but we were slow to do things, and we were jealous and were always jumping up to shout and fight. So the Irishman used to wipe his hot red face and call us bad names. He told the Lithuanian not to say these names to us, but Jonidas heard them, and in his saloon, where we all went down after the meeting when the Irishman was gone, Jonidas gave us free drinks and then told us the names. I will not write them here.

One night that Irishman did not come and Jonidas saw his chance and took the chair. He talked very fine and we elected him President. We made him Treasurer, too. Down in the saloon he gave us free drinks and told us we must break away from the Irish grafters. The next week he made us strike, all by himself. We met twice a day in his saloon and spent all of our money on drinks and then the strike was over. I got out of this union after that. I had been working hard in the cattle killing room and I had a better job. I was called a cattle butcher now and I joined the Cattle Butchers' Union. This union is honest and it has done me a great deal of good. It has raised my wages. The man who worked at my job before the union came was getting through the year an average of $9 a week. I am getting $11. In my first job I got $5 a week. The man who works there now gets $5.75.

It has given me more time to learn to read and speak and enjoy life like an American. I never work now from 6 a.m. to 9 p.m. and then be idle the next day. I work now from 7 a.m. to 5.30 p.m., and there are not so many idle days. The work is evened up.

With more time and more money I live much better and I am very happy. So is Alexandria. She came a year ago and has learned to speak English already. Some of the women go to the big store the day they get here, when they have not enough sense to pick out the clothes that look right, but Alexandria waited three weeks till she knew, and so now she looks the finest of any woman in the district. We have four nice rooms, which she keeps very clean, and she has flowers growing in boxes in the two front windows. We do not go much to church, because the church seems to be too slow. But we belong to a Lithuanian society that gives two picnics in summer and two big balls in winter, where we have a fine time. I go one night a week to the Lithuanian Concertina Club. On Sundays we go on the trolley out into the country.

But we like to stay at home more now because we have a baby. When he grows up I will not send him to the Lithuanian Catholic school. They have only two bad rooms and two priests, who teach only in Lithuanian from prayer books. I will send him to the American school, which is very big and good. The teachers there are Americans and they belong to the Teachers' Labor Union, which has three thousand teachers and belongs to our Chicago Federation of Labor. I am sure that such teachers will give him a good chance.

Our union sent a committee to Springfield last year and they passed a law which prevents boys and girls below sixteen from working in the stockyards.

We are trying to make the employers pay on Saturday night in cash. Now they pay in checks and the men have to get money the same night to buy things for Sunday, and the saloons cash checks by thousands. You have to take one drink to have the check cashed. It is hard to take one drink.

The union is doing another good thing. It is combining all the nationalities. The night I joined the Cattle Butchers' Union I was led into the room by a negro member. With me were Bohemians, Germans and Poles, and Mike Donnelly, the President, is an Irishman. He spoke to us in English and then three interpreters told us what he said. We swore to be loyal to our union above everything else except the country, the city and the State—to be faithful to each other—to protect the women workers—to do our best to understand the history of the labor movement, and to do all we could to help it on. Since then I have gone there every two weeks and I help the movement by being an interpreter for the other Lithuanians who come in. That is why I have learned to speak and write good English. The others do not need me long. They soon learn English, too, and when they have done that they are quickly becoming Americans.

But the best thing the union does is to make me feel more

independent. I do not have to pay to get a job and I cannot be discharged unless I am no good. For almost the whole 30,000 men and women are organized now in some one of our unions and they all are directed by our central council. No man knows what it means to be sure of his job unless he has been fired like I was once without any reason being given.

So this is why I joined the labor union. There are many better stories than mine, for my story is very common. There are thousands of immigrants like me. Over 300,000 immigrants have been organized in the last three years by the American Federation of Labor. The immigrants are glad to be organized if the leaders are as honest as Mike Donnelly is. You must get money to live well, and to get money you must combine. I cannot bargain alone with the Meat Trust. I tried it and it does not work.

My young brother came over three weeks ago, to escape being sent out to fight in Japan. I tried to have my father come, too, but he was too old. I wish that ugly little shoemaker would come. He would make a good walking delegate.

Chicago, Ill.

The Chicago Strike: A Teamster

person who drives teams or a truck for hauling, esp as an occupation

Labor violence erupted again in Chicago in 1905, the year of the bloody teamsters' strike. With new-found pride and craft-consciousness, the union members decided to assert their solidarity in a strike against some of the city's mammoth wholesale and retail establishments. *lg elephant like*

But pride in being a teamster was a recent phenomenon. "Only since the year 1902," wrote the labor economist and historian John R. Commons during the 1905 strike, "have the teamsters of Chicago discovered their power. They have always been classed as unskilled labor, and the old-line trade-unionists [had] ridiculed . . . the organizers who ventured to create a teamsters' union." But in 1902 the Chicago teamsters' union, which was "never influential and often comatose," shook off its lethargy and took several momentous steps.[1] *formerly* *without an alliance* First of all, it seceded from its international organization, the Team Drivers' Union of the American Federation of Labor. The Team Drivers' Union admitted to membership not only team drivers but also team owners; the only limitation was that a team owner could own no more than five teams. The Chicago teamsters, however, refused to admit such owners to membership, arguing that owners were more concerned about fares charged than wages paid. The Chicago union limited membership to employees and to drivers who owned only the teams they drove themselves. In addition, the union began to organize the livery drivers employed by the city's major businesses. Finally, the teamsters began to express their pride in themselves as craftsmen. A "good teamster," boasted the driver-author of "The Chicago Strike," "must possess certain qualifications that every ordinary 'laborer' does not possess." He must be able to read and write, and he must have a thorough knowledge of the city's

Independent, LIX (July 6, 1905), 15-20.
1. John R. Commons, "Types of Labor Organization—The Teamsters of Chicago," *Quarterly Journal of Economics,* XIX (May 1905), 400.

geography; being bonded, he must be honest, and he "must know what to do in an emergency if anything happens to his horse or wagon." Having discovered some of their power as a united group, the Chicago teamsters were also in the process of discovering their self-worth as craftsmen. "Even the ordinary teamster," Commons observed, "looks upon his occupation as a craft, and the object of his union is to have it recognized as such."[2]

In April 1905, the drivers for Montgomery Ward and Company walked off their jobs. Soon other teamster locals and other businesses joined the conflict, which grew to be city-wide and became vicious and bloody. Lasting over three months, the strike resulted in about twenty deaths and more than four hundred serious injuries. Plaguing the union were corruption in its leadership and, as in the 1904 stockyards strike, black strikebreakers. Just days after the initial walkout, trainloads of black men began arriving in Chicago, and they were met with violence.

Moreover, it was evident that in 1905 new elements had entered into the relationship between labor conflict and racial violence in Chicago. In this dispute, unlike the stockyards strike of eight months before, the hostility of striking whites toward strikebreaking blacks had been generalized into a hatred of the black race as a whole. It did not matter whether a black victim was a strikebreaker or not; black skin had become the enemy's badge and any black person was a potential target. In one incident, a black union member was pelted with rocks; when he called out to his attackers that he was union and that his employer was not involved in the strike, one of them replied that being a "nigger," he deserved a beating anyhow. "You have the negroes in here to fight us," the teamsters' president told the employers' association, "and we answer that we have the right to attack them wherever found."[3]

Heightened group consciousness, based not only on race but also on social and economic class, was a crucial element in the strike. As Graham Taylor, a perceptive settlement-house manager, observed, the "great intensity of class consciousness" in the teamsters' strike had forged a firm bond among strikers and their families, neighbors, other wage-earners, and even the little children who supported them

2. *Ibid.,* 431.
3. Quoted in William M. Tuttle, Jr., *Race Riot: Chicago in the Red Summer of 1919* (New York, 1970), 121-22.

by hurling rocks at the strikebreakers.[4] Armed with "clubs of enormous size," the Polish wives of teamsters made fierce attacks on any strikebreaker who presumed to occupy the driver's seat that "belongs to my man." Another example of heightened white working-class solidarity was the sympathy strike conducted by hundreds of grade school students. Protesting the delivery of coal at school buildings by black strikebreakers, the students organized a "skilled pupils' " union. "We are on strike. Hurrah for the unions," read the paper badges of the students who threw bricks, stones, and pieces of wood at classmates who refused to join the picket line. Many parents supported the students' strike, some asserting that they would never permit their children to return to school so long as scabs continued to deliver coal. Even teachers encouraged the strikers. "I will invite the pupils to strike," one principal said, "if the dirty niggers deliver coal at this school."[5] *group of persons stimuli ea. other to excitement*

Further violence erupted in mid-May. An eleven-year-old white boy died of gunshot wounds on May 16, after two black strikebreakers had fired into a group of jeering children. Hysteria swept the neighborhood as enraged mobs hunted for blacks, and as blacks demonstrated their determination to defend themselves. On the evening of May 20 whites paraded in the streets proclaiming their intention of "driving the blacks off the face of the earth," but they encountered resistance when a black strikebreaker shot to death one of the marchers. And in the "black belt," where blacks marched down the streets crying "Justice" and "Down with white trash," white people were chased and beaten.[6] Labor conflict, it was readily apparent, could easily escalate into racial violence with bloody acts being perpe- *performed.* trated by both sides. *excused.*

AFTER I had worked as cash boy when a little *boy* chap, left an orphan, I improved my chances by becoming a grocer's clerk. I had by that time grown to be quite a chunk of a lad, and my new job included the delivery of goods with the grocer's wagon. I took care of my horses and the barn and became very much attached to the animals.

4. Graham Taylor, *Chicago Commons through Forty Years* (Chicago, 1936), 118.
5. *Chicago Daily Tribune,* May 12-24, 1905.
6. *Ibid.,* May 17, 19, 21-23, 1905.

One of the horses was my particular pet. He would permit no famliarity from anybody but me. He knew me, my step and voice and would prance about in his stall when I came in the morning, lay back his ears and show his big, strong teeth in a way that to others would have been a danger signal but to me meant his morning salutation. I would go fearlessly into his stall, pat his flank and shoulder and neck, ending by feeding him a lump of sugar. He sulked and was stubborn when driven by any one else, but for me would do anything I asked. He seemed to understand when I talked to him. I guess most horses must understand me, for they are all my friends.

I worked for the grocer seven years; got up between 5 and 6 in the morning, looked after the horses, had my breakfast and was out with my wagon soon after 7. I frequently did not get through until 9 or 10 at night, but I liked the work and my employer was a good man. He paid me $6 a week and boarded me. It was really the only home I had had since my early boyhood, so when the grocer failed in business I felt as sorry over it as he did himself.

I next got a job with a department store, first as helper and afterward as driver. About that time the teamsters formed a union and I became a charter member of the delivery wagon drivers' branch. Through the influence of the union we got a regular scale of wages, the first year $12 a week and after two and a half years $15 a week as the minimum. We have nothing to do with the care of the horses. When a wagon is taken to the barn afer the day's work is finished the "inside" men take charge and we have nothing further to do until the next morning, when we find our teams hitched, ready waiting for us to start right out.

I make one exception to the regular rule, however. I go to the barn a while before leaving time and personally grease my wagon. My reason for this is because I want it to run without grinding. I have learned just what attention the wagon requires and I find I can do the greasing more satisfactorily myself. After I have fixed it up the wheels run along easily and without "catching." A driver gets to know his wagon, what it requires and what it can do, just as a locomotive engineer knows his engine.

If there is a hitch anywhere he recognizes the cause of the trouble at once; so sensitive does a driver become to the smooth running of his wagon that he can actually tell the instant a boy catches hold of the tailboard as he drives along the street. That little additional drag is felt by the man on the seat just as certainly as it is by the horse in the shafts.

The union not only regulated wages and working hours, but improved the class of men employed. We of the Delivery Wagons' Union are under bonds, and on account of the responsibility attached to the work we exercise care in admitting men to our organization. We frequently have the collection of C.O.D. bills, so it is to our own interest to have honest and reliable men. One man going wrong brings the whole organization into disrepute. I can see trouble ahead in getting back to our former standard when the strike ends.

Now, about this strike. The teamsters of Chicago are subdivided into over fifty different unions. Each branch of the work has its separate organization. There are over 35,000 teamsters enrolled, and at the height of the trouble something less than 10,000 drivers, helpers and boys became involved. If less than one-third of our number have been able to kick up all the fuss we are charged with, it is interesting to conjecture what might have been done if the entire number had taken an active part.

The strike started to compel Montgomery Ward & Co. to arbitrate the causes leading up to the walk-out of their garment workers. The teamsters, being a powerful organization, voted to help the garment workers and to refuse either to haul from the boycotted firm or to deliver goods to them. That naturally led to including in the boycott houses that insisted on their drivers delivering to strike-bound houses. Drivers for coal dealers, express companies, department stores, lumber firms and many wholesale houses were from time to time added to the boycott list. Ward & Co. would not yield to the demand for arbitration of the garment workers' difficulty, claiming that the workers left their employ voluntarily nearly a year ago and that the places left vacant had been filled at once and in a satisfactory manner. As the strike progressed the garment workers' grievance became rather lost sight of in the greater question of holding the teamsters' unions together.

Many things have occurred to hurt our side of the fight. I will not admit that all the things charged against us, directly, are true, but at the same time I must admit that many, many things can have no defense. When the Employers' Association formed a teaming company and offered to put their men to work in the places of the strikers they brought to Chicago for that purpose a lot of non-union drivers, some of them pretty tough customers. The new drivers for coal teams were mostly negroes from Southern cities, and they had nerve to stay on their wagons in spite of persuasion to give up. Then some of the overzealous union drivers, assisted by sympathizers, who regarded force a better argument than mere words, undertook to dispose of these strike-breakers. Every union driver conceived it to be his privilege, if not duty, to block the way of the "scabs." One thing led to another until stones and bricks were freely thrown at the imported drivers. The officers of one of the local unions took part in the forcible style of argument, and their arrest followed.

It was charged in the hearing before the grand jury that a gang of fighters, known as the "Educational Committee," was employed to "do" certain drivers. A man would be spotted and when the chance came he would be attacked by the "Educational Committee." In some instances he would not recover from the beating, and in other cases he would be crippled for life. That sort of thing, of course, instead of doing our cause any good injured us with the public and caused discontent in our own ranks. Many of us are bitterly opposed to any such methods.

It got so that a man really carried his life in his hands when he started out to drive a team for a boycotted firm, if he happened to come in contact with a crowd of these "educators" without being amply protected by a police guard.

When the strike extended to the lumber drivers there was all sorts of trouble over in the West Side lumber district. A large number of the union drivers are Poles—Polaks, they are commonly called—and they live in small houses in the vicinity. Their women are big and strong. It is no unusual sight to see one of these women carrying, with apparently little effort, a load of firewood or huge sack of coal that would stagger an ordinary man. They know but little English, but constantly are chattering in the strange lingo of their native land. When their husbands and sons left their jobs and a new set took their places those women at once took a hand in the effort to drive away the men they regarded as interlopers. They knew little if anything about any conflict between the unions and employers. All that any one of them could understand was that a stranger sat on the lumber wagon that "belongs to my man." That was not to be tolerated for a moment. Armed with heavy clubs they charged on the non-union drivers, and unless the police guard was strong enough to cope with infuriated amazons it went pretty hard with the drivers if the women got within reach of them with their clubs.

In all the riotous scenes attending the strike there was nothing done even to approach the fierceness of the attacks by these women. The police would charge upon them with drawn clubs, but hesitated when it came to rapping them over the head as they would have done in the case of dispersing a mob of men. The officers would content themselves with laying vigorous licks on the well-developed part of the muscular women's anatomy presenting the most promising target, without accomplishing much more than drawing the "fire" of the attacking party to themselves. Many a time drivers, policemen and bystanders would be compelled to flee pellmell before a mob of these women, flourishing clubs of enormous size.

A favorite way to oppose the strike-breakers at the lumber yards was to set fire to their loads. A can of oil poured over the rear of the load and a lighted match did the work. In spite of the vigilance of the guards, the loads frequently would be set on fire, and, of course the sight of a load of burning lumber soon attracted a big crowd.

The attacks next hardest to handle by the police were those engaged in by school children. These young sympathizers soon picked up the spirit of lawlessness. At the public schools when a non-union driver brought a load of coal for the building the children, only too pleased to have a chance to yell and get into mischief, hooted at the drivers, finally going to the extent of throwing stones at them. It was only by the aid of parents that the police at last were able to put a stop to these outbreaks.

But far the greatest blow our cause received was the discovery that some of our leaders were engaged in the most disreputable mode of life. They spent nights in low resorts and spent money freely in entertaining women of the vilest character. On top of all this it was openly charged that some of these officers had been receiving money from certain employers, either for the purpose of calling a strike or to settle one. The only offset to these damaging stories lay in the fact that the paying employers were equally to blame.

As already stated, many of us are opposed to violence and to the destruction of property. I, for one, think the cause of unionism has received a blow that will take some time to recover from. These lawless acts were practiced by a bad element in our own ranks, I am sorry to say, but were largely participated in by a lot of hoodlums, who took advantage of conditions to defy the law. Teamsters are not all angels, any more than are all men engaged in other lines of work, but in our ranks we have some good law-abiding citizens, who will compare favorably with the best. We have been charged with things of which I feel sure none of us have been guilty. For instance, we have been charged with throwing acid on horses driven by non-union drivers. I would not be afraid to wager my life that no teamster worthy the name ever did such a dastardly thing. Why, we fairly love horses, and I know if anybody attempted to hurt my horses I would be down off my wagon in a jiffy with my coat off ready to fight. I cannot deny that acid "eggs" were thrown at horses at times, but it couldn't have been done by teamsters.

It has been said that driving a team is not a trade and that teamsters should not be classed as trade unionists. It may not be a trade in the sense that, say, carpenter work or printing is, but still a good teamster must possess certain qualifications that every ordinary "laborer" does not possess. In our union a member must serve three years before he can receive the highest wages of the scale. He must read and write and know the city thoroughly. He must know what to do in an emergency if anything happens to his horse or wagon. His horse may pick up a nail, take sick, go lame, or show distress from any cause. If the driver is capable he knows what to do for the time being. If the harness break or the wagon meet with an accident, he must be able to patch up the one and make shift with the other.

I heard of a non-union driver, during the early days of the strike, who broke a shaft by running into something way out on the southside. When a crowd gathered around and laughed at his mishap, he seemed to be perfectly helpless. He simply took to his heels and left his wagon on the hands of his police guard. The officer had to tie up the shaft with a strap, take the outfit to a neighboring livery stable and telephone for another driver. I also heard that the darky driver had collected $40 on a C.O.D. before the accident.

I refer to this incident to indicate the difference between trained and trusty drivers and pick-ups.

From present indications the strike soon will be over. I am both sorry and glad—sorry that it was so badly managed, but glad that we will have the chance to get work again at living wages. I am quite sick of living on the "benefit."

Some of us, most likely, will not get our old jobs back in a hurry, but then—well, we'll have to make the best of it.

Chicago, Ill.

A Cap Maker's Story: Rose Schneiderman

Unlike the other undistinguished Americans in this book, Rose Schneiderman would not remain just another anonymous American working woman. Her career as feminist and labor leader stretched over more than half a century, as she went from union organizer to president of the New York Women's Trade Union League to secretary of the New York Department of Labor. Sixty-two years after starting her autobiography in the *Independent,* she completed it in *All for One* (New York, 1967).

The *Independent* article was written by a young woman growing conscious of class and sexual bonds, and beginning to define herself within American society. Born in Saven, Poland, into a religious Jewish family, Schneiderman came to the United States at age eight in 1890. Upon her arrival her name was Americanized from Rochel (Rachel) to Rose. In this article she described her first involvement in organizing women workers, and how, after organizing the plant in which she worked, she became an officer of the local union. In 1904, when she was twenty-two years old, she joined the union's General Executive Board, the first woman elected to such a high union position in the United States.

Schneiderman was part of a new breed of feminists, dedicated to improving the conditions of women and to gaining appreciation for women's roles outside of the home. Schneiderman herself was most comfortable in a woman's world, but not in the stereotyped domestic role. Her social awareness had been stirred by close friends of an aunt and uncle who were socialists, and by Bessie Brout, a coworker who "talked organization" and helped her crystalize these ideas. Schneiderman learned of the potential power of women when she and the other young women organized their shop without any help or support from the male workers. She then committed the rest of her life to working for and organizing women.

Independent, LVIII (Apr. 27, 1905), 935-38.

She found her work in the "movements"—labor and feminist—personally satisfying. She discovered that her first union office provided her with a sense of mission and purpose: "all of a sudden I was not lonely anymore," she recalled in her memoirs. She never married, and had a sense that she had chosen between a conventional life and the life of an activist. At the same time, she found personal reward in a world of female companions. Her early experiences, as related in "A Cap Maker's Story," reveal the growing self-awareness of a feminist at the turn of the century—not a mature activist with carefully thought-out ideas and conceptions, but a young woman in the process of forming ideas and direction.

MY NAME is Rose Schneiderman, and I was born in some small city of Russian Poland. I don't know the name of the city, and have no memory of that part of my childhood. When I was about five years of age my parents brought me to this country and we settled in New York.

So my earliest recollections are of living in a crowded street among the East Side Jews, for we also are Jews.

My father got work as a tailor, and we lived in two rooms on Eldridge Street, and did very well, though not so well as in Russia, because mother and father both earned money, and here father alone earned the money, while mother attended to the house. There were then two other children besides me, a boy of three and one of five.

I went to school until I was nine years old, enjoying it thoroughly and making great progress, but then my father died of brain fever and mother was left with three children and another one coming. So I had to stay at home to help her and she went out to look for work.

A month later the baby was born, and mother got work in a fur house, earning about $6 a week and afterward $8 a week, for she was clever and steady.

I was the house worker, preparing the meals and looking after the other children—the baby, a little girl of six years, and a boy of nine. I managed very well, tho the meals were not very elaborate. I could cook simple things like porridge, coffee and eggs, and mother used to prepare the meat before she went away in the morning, so that all I had to do was to put it in the pan at night.

The children were not more troublesome than others, but this was a hard part of my life with few bright spots in it. I was a serious child, and cared little for children's play, and I knew nothing about the country, so it was not so bad for me as it might have been for another. Yet it was bad, tho I did get some pleasure from reading, of which I was very fond: and now and then, as a change from the home, I took a walk in the crowded street.

Mother was absent from half-past seven o'clock in the morning till half-past six o'clock in the evening.

I was finally released by my little sister being taken by an aunt, and the two boys going to the Hebrew Orphan Asylum, which is a splendid institution, and turns out good men. One of these brothers is now a student in the City College, and the other is a page in the Stock Exchange.

When the other children were sent away mother was able to send me back to school and I stayed in this school (Houston Street Grammar) till I had reached the Sixth Grammar Grade.

Then I had to leave in order to help support the family. I got a place in Hearn's as cash girl, and after working there three weeks changed to Ridley's, where I remained for two and a half years. I finally left because the pay was so very poor and there did not seem to be any chance of advancement, and a friend told me that I could do better making caps.

So I got a place in the factory of Hein & Fox. The hours were from 8 a.m. to 6 p.m., and we made all sorts of linings—or, rather, we stitched in the linings—golf caps, yachting caps, etc. It was piece work, and we received from 3½ cents to 10 cents a dozen, according to the different grades. By working hard we could make an average of about $5 a week. We would have made more but had to provide our own machines, which cost us $45, we paying for them on the installment plan. We paid $5 down and $1 a month after that.

I learned the business in about two months, and then made as much as the others, and was consequently doing quite well when the factory burned down, destroying all our machines—150 of them. This was very hard on the girls who had paid for their machines. It was not so bad for me, as I had only paid a little of what I owed.

Rose Schneiderman, a cap maker, is shown at her sewing machine. She left the sweatshop to organize women workers, and became a leader in the women's trade union movement. By permission of Tamiment Library, New York University.

The bosses got $500,000 insurance, so I heard, but they never gave the girls a cent to help them bear their losses. I think they might have given them $10, anyway,

Soon work went on again in four lofts, and a little later I became assistant sample maker. This is a position which, tho coveted by many, pays better in glory than in cash. It was still piece work, and tho the pay per dozen was better the work demanded was of a higher quality, and one could not rush through samples as through the other caps. So I still could average only about $5 per week.

After I had been working as a cap maker for three years it began to dawn on me that we girls needed an organization. The men had organized already, and had gained some advantages, but the bosses had lost nothing, as they took it out of us.

We were helpless; no one girl dare stand up for anything alone. Matters kept getting worse. The bosses kept making reductions in our pay, half a cent a dozen at a time. It did not sound important, but at the end of the week we found a difference.

We didn't complain to the bosses; we didn't say anything except to each other. There was no use. The bosses would not pay any attention unless we were like the men and could make them attend.

One girl would say that she didn't think she could make caps for the new price, but another would say that she thought she could make up for the reduction by working a little harder, and then the first would tell herself:

"If she can do it, why can't I?"

They didn't think how they were wasting their strength.

A new girl from another shop got in among us. She was Miss Bessie Brout, and she talked organization as a remedy for our ills. She was radical and progressive, and she stimulated thoughts which were already in our minds before she came.

Finally Miss Brout and I and another girl went to the National Board of United Cloth Hat and Cap Makers when it was in session, and asked them to organize the girls.

They asked us:

"How many of you are there willing to be organized?"

"In the first place about twelve," we said. We argued that the union label would force the bosses to organize their girls, and if there was a girls' union in existence the bosses could not use the union label unless their girls belonged to the union.

We were told to come to the next meeting of the National Board, which we did, and then received a favorable answer, and were asked to bring all the girls who were willing to be organized to the next meeting, and at the next meeting, accordingly, we were there twelve strong and were organized.

When Fox found out what had happened he discharged Miss Brout, and probably would have discharged me but that I was a sample maker and not so easy to replace. In a few weeks we had all the girls in the organization, because the men told the girls that they must enter the union or they would not be allowed to work in the shop. bargain

Then came a big strike. Price lists for the coming season were given in to the bosses, to which they did not agree. After some wrangling a strike was declared in five of the biggest factories. There are 30 factories in the city. About 100 girls went out.

The result was a victory, which netted us—I mean the girls—$2 increase in our wages on the average.

All the time our union was progressing very nicely. There were lectures to make us understand what trades unionism is and our real position in the labor movement. I read upon the subject and grew more and more interested, and after a time I became a member of the National Board, and had duties and responsibilities that kept me busy after my day's work was done.

But all was not lovely by any means, for the bosses were not at all pleased with their beating and had determined to fight us again.

They agreed among themselves that after the 26th of December, 1904, they would run their shops on the "open" system.

This agreement was reached last fall, and soon notices, reading as follows, were hung in the various shops:

NOTICE

After the 26th of December, 1904, this shop will be run on the open shop system, the bosses having the right to engage and discharge employees as they see fit, whether the latter are union or nonunion.

Of course, we knew that this meant an attack on the union. The bosses intended gradually to get rid of us, employing in our place child labor and raw immigrant girls who would work for next to nothing.

On December 22nd the above notice appeared, and the National Board, which had known about it all along, went into session prepared for action.

Our people were very restive, saying that they could not sit under that notice, and that if the National Board did not call them out soon they would go out of themselves.

At last word was sent out, and at 2.30 o'clock all the workers stopped, and, laying down their scissors and other tools, marched out, some of them singing the "Marseillaise."

We were out for thirteen weeks, and the girls established their reputation. They were on picket duty from seven o'clock in the morning till six o'clock in the evening, and gained over many of the nonunion workers by appeals to them to quit working against us.

Our theory was that if properly approached and talked to few would be found who would resist our offer to take them into our organization. No right thinking person desires to injure another. We did not believe in violence and never employed it.

During this strike period we girls each received $3 a week; single men $3 a week, and married men $5 a week. This was paid us by the National Board.

We were greatly helped by the other unions, because the open shop issue was a tremendous one, and this was the second fight which the bosses had conducted for it.

Their first was with the tailors, whom they beat. If they now could beat us the outlook for unionism would be bad.

Some were aided and we stuck out, and won a glorious victory all along the line. That was only last week. The shops are open now for all union hands and for them only.

While the strike lasted I tried to get work in a factory that was not affected, but found that the boss was against me.

Last spring I had gone as a member of a committee to appeal to this boss on behalf of a girl who had been four years in his employ and was only getting $7 a week. She wanted $1 raise and all legal holidays. Previously she had had to work on holidays. After argument we secured for her the $1 raise and half a day on every legal holiday.

When the strike broke out, looking for work, I went to this boss, and he stared at me, and said:

"What do you want?"

"You asked for a girl."

"You—you—I don't want you," said he. "Can't I have my choice?"

"Certainly," said I, "I could never work where I'm not wanted."

I suppose he expected me to revenge myself by keeping other girls away, but I sent him others till he filled the place.

He resented my having served on the committee, and so he did not want me, but I felt honored by the manner in which I was treated. It showed that I had done my duty.

The bosses try to represent this open shop issue as tho they were fighting a battle for the public, but really it is nothing of the sort. The open shop is a weapon to break the unions and set men once more cutting each other's throats by individual competition.

Why, there was a time in the cap trade when men worked fourteen hours a day, and then took the heads of their machines home in bags and setting them up on stands, put mattresses underneath to deaden the sound and worked away till far into the morning.

We don't want such slavery as that to come back.

The shops are open now for all union people, and all nonunion people can join the union. In order to take in newcome foreigners we have for them cut the initiation fees down to one-half what we Americans have to pay, and we trust them till they get work and their wages.

In order to give the newcomers a chance we have stopped night work, which doesn't suit the bosses, because it causes them to pay more rent when they can't use their buildings night and day. It costs them the price of another loft instead of costing the workers their health and lives as in the old days.

Our trade is well organized, we have won two victories and are not going backward.

But there is much to be done in other directions. The shop girls certainly need organization, and I think that they ought to be easy to organize, as their duties are simple and regular and they have a regular scale of wages.

Many saleswomen on Grand and Division streets, and, in fact, all over the East Side, work from 8 a.m. till 9 p.m. week days, and one-half a day on Sundays for $5 and $6 a week; so they certainly need organization.

The waitresses also could easily be organized, and perhaps the domestic servants. I don't know about stenographers. I have not come in contact with them.

Women have proved in the late strike that they can be faithful to an organization and to each other. The men give us the credit of winning the strike.

Certainly our organization constantly grows stronger, and the Woman's Trade Union League makes progress.

The girls and women by their meetings and discussions come to understand and sympathize with each other, and more and more easily they act together.

It is the only way in which they can hope to hold what they now have or better present conditions.

Certainly there is no hope from the mercy of the bosses.

Each boss does the best he can for himself with no thought of the other bosses, and that compels each to gouge and squeeze his hands to the last penny in order to make a profit.

So we must stand together to resist, for we will get what we can take—just that and no more.

New York, March 20, 1905

The Autobiography of a Labor Leader: James Williams

something from formal, appearing present

Even at the turn of the twentieth century, a seaman's work and living environments were anachronisms from an earlier time. Most of the merchant marine, especially the coastal trade, used sailing vessels that differed from eighteenth-century ships in size only. The world of topsails and yardarms had not changed, nor had life below decks with its cramped conditions and inadequate diet. On board and in the harbor, life had changed little in a century; on ship, captains had absolute power; on shore, seamen lived a violent life, exploited by crimps—illegal labor agents—boardinghouse owners, and others. Andrew Furuseth's leadership of the Coast Seamen's Union on the West Coast, the union's fight against the shipping owners, and its lobbying efforts for federal and state legislation to protect seamen helped dramatize the brutalizing conditions that seamen encountered. The growth of the American empire and of foreign trade in the late nineteenth century also served to focus attention on the merchant marine, since Captain Alfred Thayer Mahan's theories of seapower gained wide aceptance at this time and Mahan had argued that the merchant seamen were links in the chain of empire.

James Williams was an organizer of American coastal seamen in the Atlantic ports. Labor organizing required a great deal of courage and ability, especially in the harbor or on the waterfront. It required the versatility both to testify before government commissions and to fight scabs. In the depression days of the Boston strike of 1894, for instance, shipowners had no difficulty recruiting scabs, and Williams and other seamen did not hesitate to use violence to discourage the scabs from reporting to work.

James Williams wrote extensively in popular journals, articulating the experiences and victimization of ordinary seamen. His writings

Independent, LIV (Nov. 6, 1902), 2634-38.

have been collected by Warren F. Kuehl in *Blow the Man Down!* (New York, 1959). Williams remained a seaman and union man all his life, and died in Sailor's Snug Harbor, the seamen's retirement home overlooking New York Bay, in 1947.

What set Williams apart from the majority of seamen was that he was a black man. Nowhere in this or other *Independent* articles did Williams hint at his race. Yet his organizing experience must be seen within a racial context, as a black man organizing whites and blacks. Although many craft unions had become notorious for segregating or even excluding blacks at the turn of the century, in many industries where blacks were well represented, union activity became a united black-white fight from the start. The coal miners', longshoremen's, teamsters', and waiters' national unions all had black members among their founders. In many situations where blacks and whites worked together and where they realized early that bosses manipulated racial antagonisms to divide and weaken the workers, the unions were integrated efforts. Blacks had been present in the merchant marine, especially coastal shipping, for generations, both as free men and as slaves. A union without blacks could not have organized seamen effectively. In this case, as in other industries, workers were able to see clearly their own interests as working men and resist allowing the bosses to use racism to manipulate and divide them.

I DRIFTED INTO the labor movement as naturally as a ship goes with the tide or before a leading wind. I was originally endowed with a fair share of common sense, strong democratic tendencies and a sympathetic nature. I knew the tricks of the trade and sympathized with my associates in misfortune, whose sufferings I shared. I first became identified with the labor movement at Calcutta, India. All I knew of trade union tactics at that time was what I had gleaned from time to time from newspaper reports of strikes, lockouts, boycotts, labor riots, etc., and I must confess right here that I was not prejudiced in their favor.

I had not yet had an opportunity to investigate the causes which lead to such unpleasant effects. I was only a sailor, and like most others of my class had a sublime and abiding reverence for law and order, and always bowed supinely to the rules promulgated by my masters.

But there is always a point at which "patience ceases to be a virtue," and where oppression becomes the parent of rebellion. So it was in my case. I had already endured the onerous exactions and cruel conditions of the unjust American shipping system more than half my life and always noticed that the more I yielded the more I had to yield and the less thanks I got. I wanted to make a stand for what I considered my rights somehow, but did not know exactly how to proceed.

I could hand, reef and steer, box the compass or send down a royal yard, but I knew nothing of trade union principles. The conditions existing at Calcutta at that time were certainly not calculated to redound to the sailor's best interests.

As individuals we were powerless against the crimps who infested the port and who, owing to the indifference of the officials, continued to deprive us of our rights and our earnings from voyage to voyage with monotonous regularity.

I had often observed in hoisting a topsail we all pulled, not only in the same direction, but in unison and with the same purpose—to raise the yard. This idea set me thinking. If by concentrated effort we could raise a topsail yard, why could we not raise our wages by the same method?

I consulted with some of my shipmates and we decided to write to England for permission to establish a branch of the Amalgamated Sailors' and Firemen's Union in Caclutta.

We also asked the president of the Board of Trade in London to have the rules of the board enforced in Calcutta. Both requests were granted.

After a short but rather exciting period of agitation we succeeded in inducing a majority of the seamen in port to enroll in the union.

The sailor's chaplain at Caclutta then was the Reverend Father Hopkins, a Church of England minister, and since none of our members could or would accept the position we elected him secretary.

Father Hopkins had manifested much interest in our cause and entered heartily into all our plans. He always counseled us to confine our arguments among the "black legs" to moral suasion, and we

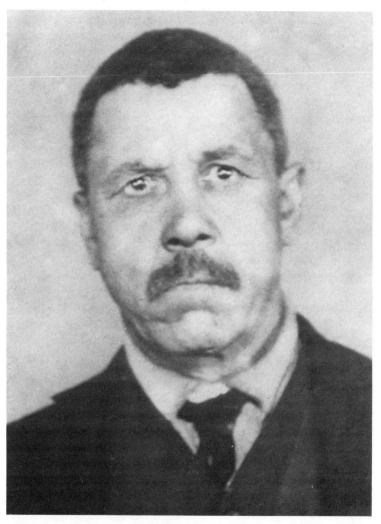

While shipping out regularly, James H. Williams, a black seaman, organized his fellow sailors and wrote articles that exposed the harsh conditions aboard Atlantic freighters. He sat for this photograph in 1919 when he applied for his Seaman's Certificate of American Citizenship. National Archives.

always did, tho sometimes with the assistance of a hardwood club.

Father Hopkins had two assistant missionaries to assist him in his work among the seamen and he permitted them to act as walking delegates for the union.

Sailors, as a rule, are prejudiced against "sky pilots" and "devil dodgers." So it was that shortly after the leading spirits of the movement had left the port the organization began to decline, and when I returned to Calcutta two years afterward it had degenerated into a guild.

A sky pilot is all right in a pulpit, but it takes a laborer to run a trade union. Altho, indirectly, I have devoted some of my attention to all seamen's unions, my direct labors among seafaring men have been confined to the men sailing on this coast. "The Atlantic Coast Seamen's Union" was organized in 1889. At that time I was homeward bound from a deep water voyage, and first heard of the movement at Demerara, B. G. On reaching the coast I made inquiries concerning the condition, purposes and policy of the union, and after consideration I decided to become a member.

I first came into prominence in 1893. In the early part of that year the sailors had succeeded, through the power of organization, in raising their wages from $16 to $30 per month, but they had made the mistake of utilizing the crimps as their principal organizers.

In December I reached Boston and found that there was a strike on. The shipowners and crimps had decided that $18 per month was enough for a man before the mast and that $2 for the chance was about the right figure. Later on the wages were further reduced to $16 per month, and the shipping fee accordingly raised to $3.

I shall never forget that terrible winter siege. At the beginning our finances were low, but as the shipowners were obliging enough to lay up about 50 per cent. of their tonnage so that union men would not have to work, and managed to sail the remainder with scabs, we were soon in sore straits. Then it was we perceived the folly of temporizing with our enemies.

We had a large meeting room at 152 Commercial Street. Besides the meeting room and office we had two large upper floors. From the middle of December, 1893, until the 10th of March, 1894, there were from 200 to 300 sailors sleeping on the hard, bare floors and benches every night. So many hungry men were hard to control, and somehow, altho our secretary was a good man, I gradually and unconsciously assumed actual charge of the situation.

The winter was an unusually severe one even for New England, and many others beside sailors were suffering from want. Soup kitchens and bean foundries were opened at various points in the poorer quarters of the city, and I often walked for miles through banks of snow in the piercing wind to find the place where I could get the largest plate of beans or the largest bowl of soup for a nickel.

I took a leading part in all the many meetings we held that winter, and, as a rule, my advice was adopted. Mass meetings were held almost daily to keep up the enthusiasm of the men. The crowd was divided into squads of four. Every morning each squad would separate, each man going in a different direction to see what he could bum. In the evening when the squads assembled each man was to share with the other members of his squad whatever he had found, borrowed or stolen. Persuasion committees were organized to watch and report, and intimidate scabs. A "hall" committee was appointed to preserve order in the hall at night and no one could gain admission after 10 p.m. Each member was required to assist in keeping the hall clean.

Thus we struggled along, until long before spring we had succeeded in practically tying up the shipping of the port. The crimps tried in every way to continue their business and we tried in every way to circumvent them.

There was one crimp who was particularly obnoxious to us. He was the most persistent and unprincipled scoundrel of them all. He kept a boarding house and was also a shipping agent—a double headed jackal. He owned a horse and wagon and was in the habit of putting crews on board vessels at night. I decided to put a stop to his night work and I did.

I induced a chum of mine to go to this man's house and board a few days, get the bearings of the house and report to me from time to time what was going on. One bitter cold evening my chum reported that a crew of scabs was to be sent away after midnight to join a vessel lying at South Boston. I told him to get the key to the barn. While he was gone I went to the office and took a sling shot from the desk and putting it in my pocket returned to my chum, who had in the meantime got the key. Then I went after a hammer and cold chisel. We unlocked the stable door and went in. After some difficulty we got the horse's shoes off. These we took, with the harness and threw over the dock. Next I took a wrench and slacked up the nuts on the wagon wheels, leaving them just on a thread. Then we locked the door. My chum returned the key to its place and went to bed. The cold was intense, but I waited patiently outside the stable until about half past one before Mr. B. came out to harness his horse. When he missed his harness his rage was really pathetic and his profanity was so extreme that I almost fancied I could smell brimstone. While he was invoking all the blessings of perdition on the sailors' union I was nearly exploding with merriment.   hell

He did not notice his horse's hoofs nor his wagon wheels until he left the stable, when his wagon got shipwrecked and he found himself and six scabs and two big policemen sitting on an ice patch at the spot where I had accidentally thrown several buckets of water the night before.

This was only one of the many tricks we played on the crimps that winter, but it is illustrative of our methods.

Mr. C. A. Walker was secretary of our union at that time, and he often urged me to accept an official position in the organization, but I declined. On March 1st, 1894, the sailors of Boston made a demand for an increase of $10 per month in wages and the abolition of shipping fees. The struggle was short but bitter, and there were many broken heads before we were through. In ten days, however, we won.

In April, 1894, I went to Providence, R. I., where we had a branch in charge of Mr. Horace Atkinson. On the day of my arrival Mr. Atkinson showed me a telegram from our New York agent advising him that a crew had been sent to his port from New York, at $7 per month below the regular wages. Next morning a committee was sent to the depot to intercept them, but failed. The men and their baggage were taken on board and the vessel, being light, hauled out into the stream. About midnight that night Mr. Atkinson and I went out in a small boat to "pull" the scabs. It was an ideal night for such a venture. There was not a breath of wind, the water was smooth and drizzling rain was falling. There was no moon.

We pulled quietly alongside the schooner, and after much difficulty I climbed over her rail at the port fore rigging and dropped on deck right abreast the forecastle door. Mr. Atkinson remained in the boat.

It was a very hazardous undertaking, as I knew the captain and mate were keeping watch on the poop and would not hesitate to shoot me if I was discovered. Besides I knew that when I gained the forecastle I would have six men to deal with single-handed.

Darkness favored me and I gained the forecastle unobserved. When I got inside the six seamen were all asleep in their bunks. I awoke them and at once began to stow their clothing in their canvas bags. They wanted to know what I was doing. I told them that there was a fleet of boats alongside loaded with union men and that I had been sent on board as a committee to notify them that unless they went quietly with me a committee of twenty would be sent on board to drag them out.

They took the bluff and proceeded to pack up with my assistance. As fast as their bags were ready I lowered them over the side one by one into the boat, where Mr. Atkinson received them. The men followed, and as we had a gun in the rowboat they made no disturbance while we rowed toward the shore. The next day the vessel shipped a crew of union men.

On July 2d, 1894, I was elected delegate to Philadelphia, Pa., while Mr. Atkinson was elected business agent at the same port. We had a strike while I was there and won it in a week.

During the strike I organized a persuasion committee, consisting of six of the best fighting men I could find—the worst cards in the pack. Whenever we learned that a non-union crew was to be signed we would go round the other way and waylay them. They were seldom eager to ship when our committee was through arguing with them.

Shortly after the strike was over I was sent to New York with instructions to close up the branch. New York had been a drain on our resources for a long time and had never paid running expenses.

On my way to New York I determined not to close the branch, as directed by headquarters, but to organize the sailors instead. I could not bear to haul down the union's colors and become the leader of an unconditional surrender.

I have always been proud of that decision, for the years that have passed by now witness the splendid condition of our union at this port.

The shipping of the port is now practically in the hands of the union and at least 95 per cent. of the coasting sailors are members of it. Besides this we have formed a Marine Firemen's Union and have already enrolled more than 2,000 marine firemen. It now requires a large staff of officers to conduct the business of the union and no one is allowed to ship except through our offices, of which there are now four. And still the good work goes on. In 1894 there were but four branches on the Atlantic Coast. Now there are eleven, while our International Union embraces some 35 locals controlled from three headquarters. And still the good work goes on and will continue to go on until we have a union as wide as the world is round, so that the sailor can be assured of good treatment, good wages and equitable conditions at any place where fortune sends him.

In January, 1899, I went to Baltimore, and arriving there with 19 cents in my pocket, succeeded, after a hard struggle, in organizing the sailors of that port, and we have a good, substantial branch there now.

I have been instrumental in breaking up the gangs of organized crimps at New York, Baltimore and Norfolk, and have done a large share of the work which preceded the enactment of the new shipping law by Congress in 1898. I was greatly assisted in this work by the Social Reform Club of New York, and my connection with the club was a liberal education to me, and I shall always remember my association with it as the pleasantest and most useful period of my life.

In May, 1895, I was sent to Albany and appeared before a Senate Committee having charge of a bill to protect seamen in New York Harbor, and in April, 1902, I was sent to Washington with a delegation to protest against the re-enactment by Congress of the Seamen's Imprisonment Bill, introduced by Mr. Allen, of Maine, last January.

At present I am an ex-officer of the union, but expect eventually to return to harness. It seems to be my life's work.

Dear reader, before you proceed to criticise these confessions, pause to investigate and do not condemn until you know.

If the shipowners and crimps would be as frank with you as I have been you might be disposed to alter your opinions in our favor. A conflict between labor and capital is an industrial war and I have never resorted to any unfair methods unless I thought the ends justified the means.

If it were not for oppression there would be no unions, and if it were not for Satan there would be no churches.

On Christmas Day when you sit before your cheerful fire at your loaded board, surrounded by your smiling wife and smiling children, with a prospect of a comfortable bed and sweet repose, please give a thought to the brave and generous men who must forego their own comfort that you may enjoy these blessings.

Think of the noble, hardy men who at that moment are rushing down through the Roaring Forties, facing the rigors and desolation of Cape Horn, running their "Easting" down or pounding their bleeding hands on frozen canvas off stormy Labrador.

The sailor is the half-brother of the world and that nation is wisest which best protects him. He has no wife to plead nor children to cry for him, therefore little is known about him.

Our merchant marine is our first line of defense. Protect your sailors and you need have no fear of a foreign invader reaching your shores. You may rest secure in the thought that all your possessions are safe and that all your wants will be supplied, for the sailor is the errand boy of the world.

The rule of the sea is the survival of the fittest, and no man will long continue to follow the sea unless he is able to fight.

New York City

A Miner's Story

The miners of the hard-coal fields of northeastern Pennsylvania had been, by the late 1890s, without a union for more than two decades. The anthracite miners' last union, the Workingmen's Benevolent Association, had succumbed in the mid-1870s, a victim of skillful union-busting by management and of the notoriety associated with the secretive and violent Molly Maguires. But in the late 1890s, the UMW United Mine Workers began to unionize the anthracite fields; and in 1900 the union won a ten percent wage increase for its members. Two years later, the UMW struck again, this time for union recognition, further wage increases, and the eight-hour day. One of the strikers, a native-born American who had worked in the mines for twenty-three of thirty-five years, outlined his grievances in the *Independent*.

Twenty-three years in the mines—fifteen of them as a miner, the rest as a child laborer—had enabled the striker to bankroll a total of $100. Gray-haired, his face lined with furrows, his lungs having accumulated years of damp air, coal dust, smoke, and powder, the miner looked and felt ten years older than he was. And yet, the striking miner lamented, financially "I am not much better off than when I started," despite having had "fairly good work since I was married" twelve years before. In addition to physical debilitation and a borderline financial existence, there was another hazard of which the miner was always fearful: accidents. The miner's brother had "struck a gas feeder," and the resultant explosion and the tons of rock and coal it dislodged had broken his bones, caused internal injuries, and "horribly burned... his whole body." And in the coal-mining industry at this time, there was no workmen's compensation, no unemployment insurance, indeed no contingency insurance of any kind. How was an anthracite miner to get ahead? And if he could get ahead, how could he secure his life against sickness, layoffs, and accidents? Perhaps the answer was a union, not that it would add substantially to his material comforts, but it might enable the miner to keep his sons in school so that they could receive an education and not at age twelve have to enter the mines and begin a life of deprivation, powerlessness, and hopelessness.

I AM thirty-five years old, married, the father of four children, and have lived in the coal region all my life. Twenty-three of these years have been spent working in and around the mines. My father was a miner. He died ten years ago from "miners' asthma."

Three of my brothers are miners; none of us had any opportunities to acquire an education. We were sent to school (such a school as there was in those days) until we were about twelve years of age, and then we were put into the screen room of a breaker to pick slate. From there we went inside the mines as driver boys. As we grew stronger we were taken on as laborers, where we served until able to call ourselves miners. We were given work in the breasts and gangways. There were five of us boys. One lies in the cemetery—fifty tons of top rock dropped on him. He was killed three weeks after he got his job as a miner—a month before he was to be married.

In the fifteen years I have worked as a miner I have earned the average rate of wages any of us coal heavers get. To-day I am little better off than when I started to do for myself. I have $100 on hand; I am not in debt; I hope to be able to weather the strike without going hungry.

I am only one of the hundreds you see on the street every day. The muscles on my arms are no harder, the callous on my palms no deeper than my neighbors' whose entire life has been spent in the coal region. By years I am only thirty-five. But look at the marks on my body; look at the lines of worriment on my forehead; see the gray hairs on my head and in my mustache; take my general appearance, and you'll think I'm ten years older.

You need not wonder why. Day in and day out, from Monday morning to Saturday evening, between the rising and the setting of the sun, I am in the underground workings of the coal mines. From the seams water trickles into the ditches along the gangways; if not water,

A miner's occupation was passed down from father to son. Most entered the mines as boys. On the other hand, because of health and safety hazards old men were rarely seen in the mines. Photo by Lewis Hine. By permission of the International Museum of Photography at George Eastman House, Rochester, N.Y.

it is the gas which hurls us to eternity and the props and timbers to a chaos.

Our daily life is not a pleasant one. When we put on our oil soaked suit in the morning we can't guess all the dangers which threaten our lives. We walk sometimes miles to the place—to the man way or traveling way, or to the mouth of the shaft on top of the slope. And then we enter the darkened chambers of the mines. On our right and on our left we see the logs that keep up the top and support the sides which may crush us into shapeless masses, as they have done to many of our comrades.

We get old quickly. Powder, smoke, after-damp, bad air—all combine to bring furrows to our faces and asthma to our lungs.

I did not strike because I wanted to; I struck because I had to. A miner—the same as any other workman—must earn fair living wages, or he can't live. And it is not how much you get that counts. It is how much what you get will buy. I have gone through it all, and I think my case is a good sample.

I was married in 1890, when I was 23 years old—quite a bit above the age when we miner boys get into double harness. The woman I married is like myself. She was born beneath the shadow of a dirt bank; her chances for school weren't any better than mine; but she did have to learn how to keep house on a certain amount of money. After we paid the preacher for tying the knot we had just $185 in cash, good health and the good wishes of many friends to start us off.

Our cash was exhausted in buying furniture for housekeeping. In 1890 work was not so plentiful, and by the time our first baby came there was room for much doubt as to how we would pull out. Low wages, and not much over half time in those years, made us hustle. In 1890-91, from June to May, I earned $368.72. That represented eleven months' work, or an average of $33.52 per month. Our rent was $10 per month; store not less than $20. And then I had my oil suits and gum boots to pay for. The result was that after the first year and a half of our married life we were in debt. Not much, of course, and not as much as many of my neighbors, men of larger families, and some who made less money, or in whose case there had been sickness or accident or death. These are all things which a miner must provide for.

I have had fairly good work since I was married. I made the average of what we contract miners are paid; but, as I said before, I am not much better off than when I started.

In 1896 my wife was sick eleven weeks. The doctor came to my house almost every day. He charged me $20 for his services. There was medicine to buy. I paid the drug store $18 in that time. Her mother nursed her, and we kept a girl in the kitchen at $1.50 a week, which cost me $15 for ten weeks, besides the additional living expenses.

In 1897, just a year afterward, I had a severer trial. And mind, in those years, we were only working about half time. But in the fall of that year one of my brothers struck a gas feeder. There was a terrible explosion. He was hurled downward in the breast and covered with the rush of coal and rock. I was working only three breasts away from him and for a moment was unable to realize what had occurred. Myself and a hundred others were soon at work, however, and in a short while we found him, horribly burned over his whole body, his laborer dead alongside of him.

He was my brother. He was single and had been boarding. He had no home of his own. I didn't want him taken to the hospital, so I directed the driver of the ambulance to take him to my house. Besides being burned, his right arm and left leg were broken, and he was hurt internally. The doctors—there were two at the house when we got there—said he would die. But he didn't. He is living and a miner to-day. But he lay in bed just fourteen weeks, and was unable to work for seven weeks after he got out of bed. He had no money when he was hurt except the amount represented by his pay. All of the expenses for doctors, medicine, extra help and his living were borne by me, except $25, which another brother gave me. The last one had none to give. Poor work, low wages and a sickly woman for a wife had kept him scratching for his own family.

It is nonsense to say I was not compelled to keep him, that I could have sent him to a hospital or the almshouse. We are American citizens and we don't go to hospitals and poorhouses.

Let us look at things as they are to-day, or as they were before this strike commenced.

My last pay envelope shows my wages, after my laborer, powder, oil and other expenses were taken off, were $29.47; that was my earnings for two weeks, and that was extra good. The laborer for the same time got some $21. His wages are a trifle over $10 a week for six full days. Before the strike of 1900 he was paid in this region $1.70 per day, or $10.20 a week. If the ten per cent. raise had been given, as we expected, his wages would be $1.87 per day, or $11.22 per week, or an increase of $1.02 per week. But we all know that under the present system he doesn't get any eleven dollars.

Well, as I said, my wages were $29.47 for the two weeks, or at the rate of $58.94 per month. My rent is $10.50 per month. My coal costs me almost $4 per month. We burn a little over a ton a month on an average and it costs us over $3 per ton. Light does not cost so much; we use coal oil altogether.

When it comes down to groceries is where you get hit the hardest. Everybody knows the cost of living has been extremely high all winter. Butter has been 32, 36 and 38 cents a pound; eggs as high as 32 cents a dozen; ham, 12 and 16 cents a pound; potatoes away up to a dollar, and cabbage not less than a cent a pound. Fresh meat need not be counted. Flour and sugar did not advance, but they were about the only staples that didn't. Anyhow, my store bill for those two weeks was $11. That makes $22 per month. The butcher gets $6 per month. Add them all, and it costs me, just to live, $42.50. That leaves me $17 per month to keep my family in clothes, to pay my church dues and to keep the industrial insurance going. My insurance alone costs me 55 cents a week, or $2.20 a month.

The coal president never allows his stable boss to cut the amount of fodder allotted to his mules. He insists on so many quarts of oats and corn to the meal and so much hay in the evening. The mule must be fed; the miner may be, if he works hard enough and earns money to buy the grub.

Company stores are of the time that has been. Their existence ended two years ago. But we've got a system growing up that threatens to be just as bad. Let me explain. Over a year ago I was given a breast to drive at one of our mines and was glad to get it. My wife took her cash and went around the different places to buy. When I went to the office for my first pay the "super" met me and asked me if I didn't know his wife's brother George kept a store. I answered, "Yes," and wanted to know what that had to do with it.

"Nothing, only I thought I'd call your attention it it," he answered.

No more was said then. But the next day I got a quiet tip that my breast was to be abandoned. This set me thinking. I went to the boss and, after a few words, told him my wife had found brother-in-law George's store and that she liked it much better than where she had bought before. I told him the other store didn't sell the right kind of silk waists, and their patent leather shoes were away back. Brother-in-law George had the right kind of stuff and, of course, we were willing to pay a few cents more to get just what we wanted.

That was sarcastic, but it's the cash that has the influence. I have had work at that colliery ever since. I know my living costs me from 10 to 15 per cent. extra. But I kept my job, which meant a good deal.

Now you must take into consideration that I am a contract miner and that my earnings are more than the wages of three-fourths of the other fellows at the same colliery. It is not that I am a favorite with the boss. I just struck a good breast. Maybe next month my wages would be from two to six or seven dollars less.

In the days of Pardee, Coxe, Fagley, Fulton, Dewees, Paterson, Riley, Replier, Graeber and a hundred others, men were better paid than they have ever been since the centralization ideas of the late Franklin B. Gowen became fixed institutions in the anthracite counties. It may be true that in the days of the individual operation the cost per ton of mining coal was less than it is to-day. But it is not right that the entire increase in the cost of mining should be charged to the miner. That is what is being done, if you count the reductions made in wages.

We miners do not participate in the high prices of coal. The operators try to prove otherwise by juggling with figures, but their proving has struck a fault, and the drill shows no coal in that section. One-half of the price paid for a ton of coal in New York or Philadelphia goes into the profit pocket of the mine owner, either as a carrier or miner.

We all know that the price of coal has advanced in the past twenty years. We also know that wages are less, that the cost of living is higher. I remember the time, when I was a wee lad, my father used to get his coal for $1 per ton. Now I pay $3. In those days we lads used to go to the dirt banks and pick a load of coal, and it cost our parents only a half a dollar to get it hauled home. We dare not do that now. Then we did not need gum boots, safety lamps or any such things as that; and for all of them we must now pay out of wages that have been reduced.

Our condition can be no worse; it might and must be better. The luxuries of the rich we do not ask; we do want butter for our bread and meat for our soup. We do not want silk and laces for our wives and daughters. But we want to earn enough to buy them a clean calico once in a while. Our boys are not expecting automobiles and membership cards in clubs of every city, but they want their fathers to earn enough to keep them at school until they have a reasonably fair education.

Pennsylvania

The Question of Race

The New Slavery in the South—
An Autobiography:
A Georgia Negro Peon

The late nineteenth century, C. Vann Woodward has written, was the period of America's "capitulation to racism." During these years at the turn of the twentieth century, the United States "betrayed" its black citizens, causing the "nadir" in the history of the nation's race relations. Beginning in the 1890s, every state in the South adopted a new constitution which disfranchised virtually every black in the region. In order to vote, a black man had to demonstrate his "understanding" of the state constitution and be of "good character"; the judge of these qualifications was usually a white registrar whose job it was to deny blacks the vote, not to register them. There was also the "grandfather clause," which extended the franchise only to those men whose grandfathers had been eligible to vote in the presidential election of 1860, a year when most blacks had been slaves. If these devices failed, poll taxes, property qualifications, and the Democratic party's whites-only primary would bar blacks. Segregation, hardly a stranger to the South, made its face known at this time in the omnipresent "Whites Only" and "Colored Only" signs that hung on the doors and walls of trains, railroad station waiting rooms, toilets, beaches, parks, libraries, saloons, and restaurants. Even the Bibles used in courtrooms were segregated, one for swearing in white witnesses, the other for blacks. Worse yet, these were years of rampant racial violence, as white mobs not only lynched blacks in record numbers but also brutalized them in riots. During the 1890s mobs lynched an average of almost 190 people per year, and at the turn of the century race riots bloodied the streets of Wilmington,

North Carolina, Phoenix, South Carolina, Atlanta, Georgia, and other cities and towns.[1]

The concluding years of the nineteenth century, Woodward has observed, constituted a period of transition in race relations, "the transition from the slavery system to the caste system. . . ."[2] The caste system, with its retinue of violence and proscription, had marched forward to succeed the institution of slavery as a means of social control, of keeping blacks in their place. In at least one way, however—peonage and convict leasing—the new system matched the oppression of the old. Practically every state in the South had enacted a contract-labor law by the twentieth century. "Under such laws," Pete Daniel has explained in his study of peonage in the South, "a laborer who signed a contract and then abandoned his job could be arrested for a criminal offense." Once arrested, the laborer faced prison and service on a chain gang. The future for such a black person was thus distressingly obvious: "he could either work out his contract or go to the chain gang."[3] In addition, contract workers—along with tenant farmers and sharecroppers—usually had little or no cash and had to buy on credit, and at exorbitant prices, from the commissaries operated by planters and other employers. At the year's end accounting, many blacks were shocked and angered to be told that they had not liquidated their indebtedness, despite dawn-to-dusk days in the fields. The indebtedness of some blacks became practically perpetual, forcing them into involuntary servitude for years and even decades. No black could question his master's annual accounting, nor could he escape except at the risk of arrest. "This simply means," Booker T. Washington explained in 1908, "that any white man, who cares to charge that a Colored man has promised to work for him and has not done so, or who has gotten money from him and not paid it back, can have the Colored man sent to the chain gang."[4] Moreover, planters and other employers in the postbellum South bought and sold their financial investments in and contracts with black people. A distinguishing difference between this commerce and slave sales was that, after emancipation, some black people were even more expend-

1. See C. Vann Woodward, *Origins of the New South, 1877-1913* (Baton Rouge, La., 1951), 205-34, 321-49.

2. *Ibid.,* 354.

3. Pete Daniel, *The Shadow of Slavery: Peonage in the South, 1901-1969* (Urbana, Ill., 1972), 25.

4. Quoted in *ibid.,* 67.

able than slaves. For example, a black man might have been convicted of a minor offense, such as vagrancy or loitering. Quite often, he would not possess the $50 or so needed to pay his fine and court costs. At this point, a white person might intercede with an offer to make the payment; by doing so, a white employer could acquire the labor of a black worker, and at an outrageously low price. Moreover, by granting credit at the commissary and/or manipulating the ledger sheets, the white could, in effect, procure the involuntary servitude of the black for years on end. That peonage was a federal crime was not a deterrent to its continued practice. Finally, the black who represented such a minimal investment would have to endure vermin-ridden barracks, food ill suited even for a draft animal, and infrequent or nonexistent medical care. After all, what could a person worth $50 expect?

The black peon whose life story follows was born in northeastern Georgia during the Civil War. In his story he described not only his agonies as a peon, but also another system of involuntary servitude—the convict-lease system. Growing up in extreme isolation from the outside world, this peon at age twenty-one signed a labor contract with "the Captain" on whose plantation he had spent his entire life. The same year he married Mandy, a servant in the captain's house, "and we set up housekeeping in one of the Captain's two-room shanties." He was happy, feeling like "the biggest man in Georgia"; he had no reason to suspect that within five years the captain's son would transform the plantation into a convict camp. Not long after the captain's death, however, his son "the Senator," a politician serving in the state legislature, "had a long, low shanty built on his place." This was the stockade, and into it one day marched "about forty able-bodied negroes, bound in iron chains, and some of them handcuffed...." These men were convicts whose labor had been leased by the senator from the state of Georgia for $200 each per year, with the state agreeing to pay for armed guards, rewards for escaped convicts, "and all other incidental camp expenses." In a few months the senator had had constructed two large sawmills, and within two years there were two hundred blacks working on the plantation, "about half of them free laborers, so-called, and about half of them convicts." Soon, however, the distinction between free (contract and/or indebted) laborer and convict became blurred. And one night the free laborers "were locked up, every one of us, in one of the Senator's stockades," and "from that day forward we were treated just like the convicts."

For three years the peon lived in one of the stockades, one of the "cesspools of nastiness"; during these years his son was "given away" to another black family, and his wife was forced by "one of the white bosses" to become his mistress. The peon's three-year imprisonment ended when "one of the bosses came to me and said that my time was up." Penniless, in ill health, and without his family, he eventually found his way to the burgeoning coal and steel industries of Birmingham, Alabama.

I AM a negro and was born some time during the war in Elbert County, Ga., and I reckon by this time I must be a little over forty years old. My mother was not married when I was born, and I never knew who my father was or anything about him. Shortly after the war my mother died, and I was left to the care of my uncle. All this happened before I was eight years old, and so I can't remember very much about it. When I was about ten years old my uncle hired me out to Captain ——. I had already learned how to plow, and was also a good hand at picking cotton. I was told that the Captain wanted me for his house-boy, and that later on he was going to train me to be his coachman. To be a coachman in those days was considered a post of honor, and, young as I was, I was glad of the chance. But I had not been at the Captain's a month before I was put to work on the farm, with some twenty or thirty other negroes—men, women and children. From the beginning the boys had the same tasks as the men and women. There was no difference. We all worked hard during the week, and would frolic on Saturday nights and often on Sundays. And everybody was happy. The men got $3 a week and the women $2. I don't know what the children got. Every week my uncle collected my money for me, but it was very little of it that I ever saw. My uncle fed and clothed me, gave me a place to sleep, and allowed me ten or fifteen cents a week for "spending change," as he called it. I must have been seventeen or eighteen years old before I got tired of that arrangement, and felt that I was man enough to be working for myself and handling my own wages. The other boys about my age and size were "drawing" their own pay, and they used to laugh at me and call me "Baby" because my old uncle was always on hand to "draw" my pay. Worked up by these things, I made a break for liberty. Unknown to my uncle or the Captain I went off to a neighboring plantation and hired myself out to another man. The new landlord agreed to give me forty cents a day and furnish me one meal. I though that was doing fine. Bright and early one Monday morning I started for work, still not letting the others know anything about it. But they found it out before sundown. The Captain came over to the new place and brought some kind of officer of the law. The officer pulled out a long piece of paper from his pocket and read it to my new employer. When this was done I heard my new boss say:

"I beg your pardon, Captain. I didn't know this nigger was bound out to you, or I wouldn't have hired him."

"He certainly is bound out to me," said the Captain. "He belongs to me until he is twenty-one, and I'm going to make him know his place."

So I was carried back to the Captain's. That night he made me strip off my clothing down to my waist, had me tied to a tree in his backyard, ordered his foreman to give me thirty lashes with a buggy whip across my bare back, and stood by until it was done. After that experience the Captain made me stay on his place night and day,—but my uncle still continued to "draw" my money.

I was a man nearly grown before I knew how to count from one to one hundred. I was a man nearly grown before I ever saw a colored school teacher. I never went to school a day in my life. To-day I can't write my own name, tho I can read a little. I was a man nearly grown before I ever rode on a railroad train, and then I went on an excursion from Elberton to Athens. What was true of me was true of hundreds of other negroes around me—'way off there in the country, fifteen or twenty miles from the nearest town.

When I reached twenty-one the Captain told me I was a free man, but he urged me to stay with him. He said he would treat me right, and pay me as much as anybody else would. The Captain's son and I were about the same age, and the Captain said that, as he had owned my mother and uncle during slavery, and as his son didn't want me to leave them (since I had been with them so long), he wanted me to stay with the old family. And I stayed. I signed a contract—that is, I made my mark—for one year. The Captain was to give me $3.50 a week, and furnish me a little house on the plantation—a one-room log cabin similar to those used by his other laborers.

During that year I married Mandy. For several years Mandy had been the house-servant for the Captain, his wife, his son and his three daughters, and they all seemed to think a good deal of her. As an evidence of their regard they gave us a suit of furniture, which cost about $25, and we set up housekeeping in one of the Captain's two-room shanties. I thought I was the biggest man in Georgia. Mandy still kept her place in the "Big House" after our marriage. We did so well for the first year that I renewed my contract for the second year, and for the third, fourth and fifth year I did the same thing. Before the end of the fifth year the Captain had died, and his son, who had married some two or three years before, took charge of the plantation. Also, for two or three years, this son had been serving at Atlanta in some big office to which he had been elected. I think it was in the Legislature or something of that sort—anyhow, all the people called him Senator. At the end of the fifth year the Senator suggested that I sign up a contract for ten years; then, he said, we wouldn't have to fix up papers every year. I asked my wife about it; she consented; and so I made a ten-year contract.

Not long afterward the Senator had a long, low shanty built on his place. A great big chimney, with a wide, open fireplace, was built at one end of it, and on each side of the house, running lengthwise, there was a row of frames or stalls just large enough to hold a single mattress. The places for these mattresss were fixed one above the other, so that there was a double row of these stalls or pens on each side. They looked for all the world like stalls for horses. Since then I have seen cabooses similarly arranged as sleeping quarters for railroad laborers. Nobody seemed to know what the Senator was fixing for. All doubts were put aside one bright day in April when about forty able-bodied negroes, bound in iron chains, and some of them handcuffed, were brought out to the Senator's farm in three big wagons. They were quartered in the long, low shanty, and it was afterward called the stockade. This was the beginning of the Senator's convict camp. These men were prisoners who had been leased by the Senator from the State of Georgia at about $200 each per year, the State agreeing to pay for guards and physicians, for necessary inspection, for inquests, all rewards for escaped convicts, the cost of litigation and all other incidental camp expenses. When I saw these men in shackles, and the guards with their guns, I was scared nearly to death. I felt like running away, but I didn't know where to go. And if there had been any place to go to, I would have had to leave my wife and child behind. We free laborers held a meeting. We all wanted to quit. We sent a man to tell the Senator about it. Word came back that we were all under contract for ten years and that the Senator would hold us to the letter of the contract, or put us in chains and lock us up— the same as the other prisoners. It was made plain to us by some white people we talked to that in the contracts we had signed we had all agreed to be locked up in a stockade at night or at any other time that our employer saw fit; further, we learned that we could not lawfully break our contract for any reason and go and hire ourselves to somebody else without the consent of our employer; and, more than that, if we got mad and ran away, we could be run down by bloodhounds, arrested without process of law, and be returned to our employer, who, according to the contract, might beat us brutally or administer any other kind of punishment that he thought proper. In other words, we had sold ourselves into slavery— and what could we do about it? The white folks had all the courts, all the guns, all the hounds, all the railroads, all the telegraph wires, all the newspapers, all the money, and nearly all the land— and we had only our ignorance, our poverty and our empty hands. We decided that the best thing to do was to shut our mouths, say nothing, and go back to work. And most of us worked side by side with those convicts during the remainder of the ten years.

But this first batch of convicts was only the beginning. Within six months another stockade was built, and twenty or thirty other convicts were brought to the plantation, among them six or eight women! The Senator had bought an additional thousand acres of land, and to his already large cotton plantation he added two great big saw-mills and went into the lumber business. Within two years the Senator had in all nearly 200 negroes working on his plantation— about half of them free laborers, so-called, and about half of them convicts. The only difference between the free laborers and the others was that the free laborers could come and go as they pleased, at night— that is, they were not locked up at night, and were not, as a general thing, whipped for slight offenses. The troubles of the free laborers began at the close of the ten-year period. To a man, they all wanted to quit when the time was up. To a man, they all refused to sign new contracts—even for one year, not to say anything of ten years. And just when we thought that our bondage was at an end we found that it had really just begun. Two or three years before, or about a year and a half after the Senator had started his camp, he had established a large store, which was called the commissary. All of us free laborers were compelled to buy our supplies—food, clothing, etc.—from that store. We never used any money in our dealings with the commissary, only tickets or orders, and we had a general settlement once each year, in October. In this store we were charged all sorts of high prices for goods, because every year we would come out in debt to our employer. If not that, we seldom had more than $5 or $10 coming to us—and that for a whole year's work. Well, at the close of the tenth year, when we kicked and meant to leave the Senator, he said to some of us with a smile (and I never will forget that smile—I can see it now):

"Boys, I'm sorry you're going to leave me. I hope you will do well in your new places—so well that you will be able to pay me the little balances which most of you owe me."

Word was sent out for all of us to meet him at the commissary at 2 o'clock. There he told us that, after we had signed what he called a written acknowledgment of our debts, we might go and look for new places. The storekeeper took us one by one and read to us statements of our accounts. According to the books there was no man of us who owed the Senator less than $100; some of us were put down for as much as $200. I owed $165, according to the bookkeeper. These debts were not accumulated during one year, but ran back for three and four years, so we were told—in spite of the fact that we understood that we had had a full settlement at the end of each year. But no one of us would have dared to dispute a white man's word—oh, no; not in those days. Besides, we fellows didn't care anything about the amounts—we were after getting away; and we had been told that we might go, if we signed the acknowledgments. We would have signed anything, just to get away. So we stepped up, we did, and made our marks. That same night we were rounded up by a constable and ten or twelve white men, who aided him, and we were locked up, every one of us, in one of the Senator's stockades. The next morning it was explained to us by the two guards appointed to watch us that, in the papers we had signed the day before, we had not only made acknowledgment of our indebtedness, but that we had also agreed to work for the Senator until the debts were paid by hard labor. And from that day forward we were treated just like convicts. Really we had made ourselves lifetime slaves, or peons, as the laws called us. But, call it slavery, peonage, or what not, the truth is we lived in a hell on earth what time we spent in the Senator's peon camp.

I lived in that camp, as a peon, for nearly three years. My wife fared better than I did, as did the wives of some of the other negroes, because the white men about the camp used these unfortunate creatures as their mistresses. When I was first put in the stockade my wife was still kept for a while in the "Big House," but my little boy, who was only nine years old, was given away to a negro family across the river in South Carolina, and I never saw or heard of him after that. When I left the camp my wife had had two children for some one of the white bosses, and she was living in fairly good shape in a little house off to herself. But the poor negro women who were not in the class with my wife fared about as bad as the helpless negro men. Most of the time the women who were peons or convicts were compelled to wear men's clothes. Sometimes, when I have seen them dressed like men, and plowing or hoeing or hauling logs or working at the blacksmith's trade, just the same as men, my heart would bleed and my blood would boil, but I was powerless to raise a hand. It would have meant death on the spot to have said a word. Of the first six women brought to the camp, two of them gave birth to children after they had been there more than twelve months—and the babies had white men for their fathers!

The stockades in which we slept were, I believe, the filthiest places in the world. They were cesspools of nastiness. During the thirteen years that I was there I am willing to swear that a mattress was never moved after it had been brought there, except to turn it over once or twice a month. No sheets were used, only dark-colored blankets. Most of the men slept every night in the clothing that they had worked in all day. Some of the worst characters were made to sleep in chains. The doors were locked and barred each night, and tallow candles were the only lights allowed. Really the stockades were but little more than cow lots, horse stables or hog pens. Strange to say, not a great number of these people died while I was there, tho a great many came away maimed and bruised and, in some cases, disabled for life. As far as I remember only about ten died during the last ten years that I was there, two of these being killed outright by the guards for trivial offenses.

It was a hard school that peon camp was, but I learned more there in a few short months by contact with those poor fellows from the outside world than ever I had known before. Most of what I learned was evil, and I now know that I should have been better off without the knowledge, but much of what I learned was helpful to me. Barring two or three severe and brutal whippings which I received, I got along very well, all things considered; but the system is damnable. A favorite way of whipping a man was to strap him down to a log, flat on his back, and spank him fifty or sixty times on his bare feet with a shingle or a huge piece of plank. When the man would get up with sore and blistered feet and an aching body, if he could not then keep up with the other men at work he would be strapped to the log again, this time face downward, and would be lashed with a buggy trace on his bare back. When a woman had to be whipped it was usually done in private, tho they would be compelled to fall down across a barrel or something of the kind and receive the licks on their backsides.

The working day on a peon farm begins with sunrise and ends when the sun goes down; or, in other words, the average peon works from ten to twelve hours each day, with one hour (from 12 o'clock to 1 o'clock) for dinner. Hot or cold, sun or rain, this is the rule. As to their meals, the laborers are divided up into squads or companies, just the same as soldiers in a great military camp would be. Two or three men in each stockade are appointed as cooks. From thirty to forty men report to each cook. In the warm months (or eight or nine months out of the year) the cooking is done on the outside, just behind the stockades; in the cold months the cooking is done inside the stockades. Each peon is provided with a great big tin cup, a flat tin pan and two big tin spoons. No knives or forks are ever seen, except those used by the cooks. At meal time the peons pass in single file before the cooks, and hold out their pans and cups to receive their allowances. Cow peas (red or white, which when boiled turn black), fat bacon and old-fashioned Georgia corn bread, baked in pones from one to two and three inches thick, make up the chief articles of food. Black coffee, black molasses and brown sugar are also used abundantly. Once in a great while, on Sundays, biscuits would be made, but they would always be made from the kind of flour called "shorts." As a rule, breakfast consisted of coffee, fried bacon, corn bread, and sometimes molasses—and one "helping" of each was all that was allowed. Peas, boiled with huge hunks of fat bacon, and a hoe-cake, as big as a man's hand, usually answered for dinner. Sometimes this dinner bill of fare gave place to bacon and greens (collard or turnip) and pot liquor. Tho we raised corn, potatoes and other vegetables, we never got a chance at such things unless we could steal them and cook them secretly. Supper consisted of coffee, fried bacon and molasses. But, altho the food was limited to certain things, I am sure we all got a plenty of the things allowed. As coarse as these things were, we kept, as a rule, fat and sleek and as strong as mules. And that, too, in spite of the fact that we had no special arrangements for taking regular baths, and no very great effort was made to keep us regularly in clean clothes. No tables were used or allowed. In summer we would sit down on the ground and eat our meals, and in winter we would sit around inside the filthy stockades. Each man was his own dish washer—that is to say, each man was responsible for the care of his pan and cup and spoons. My dishes got washed about once a week!

To-day, I am told, there are six or seven of these private camps in Georgia—that is to say, camps where most of the convicts are leased from the State of Georgia. But there are hundreds and hundreds of farms all over the State where negroes, and in some cases poor white folks, are held in bondage on the ground that they are working out debts, or where the contracts which they have made hold them in a kind of perpetual bondage, because under those contracts, they may not quit one employer and hire out to another, except by and with the knowledge and consent of the former employer. One of the usual ways to secure laborers for a large peonage camp is for the proprietor to send out an agent to the little courts in the towns and villages, and where a man charged with some petty offense has no friends or money the agent will urge him to plead guilty, with the understanding that the agent will pay his fine, and in that way save him from the disgrace of being sent to jail or the chain-gang! For this high favor the man must sign beforehand a paper signifying his willingness to go to the farm and work out the amount of the fine imposed. When he reaches the farm he has to be fed and clothed, to be sure, and these things are charged up to his account. By the time he has worked out his first debt another is hanging over his head, and so on and so on, by a sort of endless chain for an indefinite period, as in every case the indebtedness is arbitrarily arranged by the employer. In many cases it is very evident that the court officials are in collusion with the proprietors or agents, and that they divide the "graft" among themselves. As an example of this dickering among the whites, every year many convicts were brought to the Senator's camp from a certain county in South Georgia, 'way down in the turpentine district. The majority of these men were charged with adultery, which is an offense against the laws of the great and sovereign State of Georgia! Upon inquiry I learned that down in that county a number of negro lewd women were employed by certain white men to entice negro men into their houses; and then, on certain nights, at a given signal, when all was in readiness, raids would be made by the officers upon these houses, and the men would be arrested and charged with living in adultery. Nine out of ten of these men, so arrested and so charged, would find their way ultimately to some convict camp, and, as I said, many of them found their way every year to the Senator's camp while I was there. The low-down women were never punished in any way. On the contrary, I was told that they always seemed to stand in high favor with the sheriffs, constables and other officers. There can be no room to doubt that they assisted very materially in furnishing laborers for the prison pens of Georgia, and the belief was general among the men that they were regularly paid for their work. I could tell more, but I've said enough to make anybody's heart sick. I am glad that the Federal authorities are taking a hand in breaking up this great and terrible iniquity. It is, I know, widespread throughout Georgia and many other Southern States. Since Judge Speer fired into the gang last November at Savannah, I notice that arrests have been made of seven men in three different sections of the State—all charged with holding men in peonage. Somewhere, somehow, a beginning of the end should be made.

But I didn't tell you how I got out. I didn't get out—they put me out.

When I had served as a peon for nearly three years—and you remember that they claimed that I owed them only $165—when I had served for nearly three years, one of the bosses came to me and said that my time was up. He happened to be the one who was said to be living with my wife. He gave me a new suit of overalls, which cost about seventy-five cents, took me in a buggy and carried me across the Broad River into South Carolina, set me down and told me to "git." I didn't have a cent of money, and I wasn't feeling well, but somehow I managed to get a move on me. I begged my way to Columbia. In two or three days I ran across a man looking for laborers to carry to Birmingham, and I joined his gang. I have been here in the Birmingham district since they released me, and I reckon I'll die either in a coal mine or an iron furnace. It don't make much difference which. Either is better than a Georgia peon camp. And a Georgia peon camp is hell itself!

South Carolina

The Biography of a Chinaman:
Lee Chew

A native of Canton province, the source of much of the nineteenth-century Chinese immigration to the United States, Lee Chew grew up to distrust and even despise white "foreign devils," especially the English and the Americans. At the same time, he marveled at the technology of these vulgar, duplicitous, violent people—their wireless telegraphy, weapons and explosives, and steam-powered ships and spinning mills. And when he was sixteen, one of his fellow villagers returned home "with unlimited wealth, which he had obtained in the country of the American wizards." Deciding that he, too, "would like to go to the country of the wizards and gain some of their wealth," Lee Chew obtained his father's permission to emigrate.

Lee Chew debarked from his ship in San Francisco at a time of widespread and virulent anti-Chinese sentiment on the West Coast. Perceived as racially inferior, as repulsive in life-style, and as pawns of organized capital in its struggle against the workers, the Chinese in America in the 1870s and early 1880s suffered from violence and exclusion from labor unions. In California, anti-Chinese sentiment and agitation were intense and widespread in state politics, with two of its parties, the Democratic and the Workingmen's, both protesting that the Chinese were every bit as repulsive and un-American as the blacks. The Democratic party, contended the San Francisco *Examiner,* the state's foremost Democratic paper, is "for a white man's government constitutionally administered, against a great Mongrel military despotism, upheld by a union of the purse and the sword, and sought to be perpetuated through negro and Chinese votes." And Denis Kearney, an Irish immigrant and the leader of the Workingmen's party, asked his fellow workers: "Are your ready to march down to the wharf and stop the leprous Chinese from landing? . . . Judge Lynch is the judge wanted by the workingmen of California. I

Independent, LV (Feb. 19, 1903), 417-23.

advise all to own a musket and a hundred rounds of ammunition."[1]
One result of this agitation was the Chinese Exclusion Act of 1882,
which prohibited the immigration of Chinese laborers for a period of
ten years; subsequently, by treaty (in 1894) and legislative enactment
(in 1902), this prohibition was made permanent. Other results were
the looting and destruction of Chinese shops and industries, the
burning to the ground of Chinese ghettos and the dispersal of their
residents, and, on occasion, murder.

In spite of these conditions, Lee Chew was ambitious and highly
acquisitive, and he relocated frequently in his pursuit of money.
Operating laundries for a railroad construction gang and for an
assortment of hard-drinking, pistol-toting "wild men" in the gold
mines, he also established laundries successively in the Great Lakes
cities of Chicago, Detroit, and Buffalo. Finally, Lee Chew became "a
general merchant" in New York, opening an import store in the
Chinese section of the city. In the Midwest and the East, as on the
West Coast, he had to confront the harsh reality of anti-Chinese
sentiment. Viewed as opium and gambling addicts, berated as cheap,
anti-union workers, and hated as nonwhites, the Chinese in New York
and elsewhere, most of whom were unattached males, banded
together to found self-help and benevolent societies. Like other
immigrant groups which had been branded by the majority of
Americans as unassimilable—for racial, religious, or ethnic
reasons—the Chinese turned inward and found strength and support
in and among themselves.

THE VILLAGE where I was born is situated in the province of
Canton, on one of the banks of the Si-Kiang River. It is called a
village, altho it is really as big as a city, for there are about 5,000 men
it it over eighteen years of age—women and children and even youths
are not counted in our villages.

All in the village belonged to the tribe of Lee. They did not
intermarry with one another, but the men went to other villages for
their wives and and brought them home to their fathers' houses, and

---

1. Both quotations are in Alexander Saxton, "Race and the House of Labor," in
Gary B. Nash and Richard Weiss, eds., *The Great Fear: Race in the Mind of America*
(New York, 1970), 111.

men from other villages—Wus and Wings and Sings and Fongs, etc.—chose wives from among our girls.

When I was a baby I was kept in our house all the time with my mother, but when I was a boy of seven I had to sleep at nights with other boys of the village—about thirty of them in one house. The girls are separated the same way—thirty or forty of them sleeping together in one house away from their parents—and the widows have houses where they work and sleep, tho they go to their fathers' houses to eat.

My father's house is built of fine blue brick, better than the brick in the houses here in the United States. It is only one story high, roofed with red tiles and surrounded by a stone wall which also incloses the yard. There are four rooms in the house, one large living room which serves for a parlor and three private rooms, one occupied by my grandfather, who is very old and very honorable; another by my father and mother, and the third by my oldest brother and his wife and two little children. There are no windows, but the door is left open all day.

All the men of the village have farms, but they don't live on them as the farmers do here; they live in the village, but go out during the day time and work their farms, coming home before dark. My father has a farm of about ten acres, on which he grows a great abundance of things—sweet potatoes, rice, beans, peas, yams, sugar cane, pine-apples, bananas, lychee nuts and palms. The palm leaves are useful and can be sold. Men make fans of the lower part of each leaf near the stem, and water proof coats and hats, and awnings for boats, of the parts that are left when the fans are cut out.

So many different things can be grown on one small farm, because we bring plenty of water in a canal from the mountains thirty miles away, and every farmer takes as much as he wants for his fields by means of drains. He can give each crop the right amount of water.

Our people all working together make these things, the mandarin has nothing to do with it, and we pay no taxes, except a small one on the land. We have our own Government, consisting of the elders of our tribe—the honorable men. When a man gets to be sixty years of age he begins to have honor and to become a leader, and then the older he grows the more he is honored. We had some men who were nearly one hundred years, but very few of them.

In spite of the fact that any man may correct them for a fault,

An immigrant from China, Lee Chew attained financial success despite the anti-Oriental sentiment that was rampant in the United States. Chew was financially ambitious, but he also wanted to maintain Chinese customs, such as his traditional dress. Reproduced from the *Independent*.

Chinese boys have good times and plenty of play. We played games like tag, and other games like shinny and a sort of football called yin.

We had dogs to play with—plenty of dogs and good dogs—that understand Chinese as well as American dogs understand American language. We hunted with them, and we also went fishing and had as good a time as American boys, perhaps better, as we were almost always together in our house, which was a sort of boys' club house, so we had many playmates. Whatever we did we did all together, and our rivals were the boys of other club houses, with whom we sometimes competed in the games. But all our play outdoors was in the daylight, because there were many graveyards about and after dark, so it was said, black ghosts with flaming mouths and eyes and long claws and teeth would come from these and tear to pieces and devour any one whom they might meet.

It was not all play for us boys, however. We had to go to school, where we learned to read and write and to recite the precepts of Kong-foo-tsze and the other Sages and stories about the great Emperors of China, who ruled with the wisdom of gods and gave to the whole world the light of high civilization and the culture of our literature, which is the admiration of all nations.

I went to my parents' house for meals, approaching my grandfather with awe, my father and mother with veneration and my elder brother with respect. I never spoke unless spoken to, but I listened and heard much concerning the red haired, green eyed foreign devils with the hairy faces, who had lately come out of the sea and clustered on our shores. They were wild and fierce and wicked, and paid no regard to the moral precepts of Kong-foo-tsze and the Sages; neither did they worship their ancestors, but pretended to be wiser than their fathers and grandfathers. They loved to beat people and to rob and murder. In the streets of Hong Kong many of them could be seen reeling drunk. Their speech was a savage roar, like the voice of the tiger or the buffalo, and they wanted to take the land away from the Chinese. Their men and women lived together like animals, without any marriage or faithfulness and even were shameless enought to walk the streets arm in arm in daylight. So the old men said.

All this was very shocking and disgusting, as our women seldom were on the street, except in the evenings, when they went with the water jars to the three wells that supplied all the people. Then if they met a man they stood still, with their faced turned to the wall, while he looked the other way when he passed them. A man who spoke to a woman in the street in a Chinese village would be beaten, perhaps killed.

peculiar customs

My grandfather told how the English foreign devils had made wicked war on the Emperor, and by means of their enchantments and spells had defeated his armies and forced him to admit their opium, so that the Chinese might smoke and become weakened and the foreign devils might rob them of their land.

biasd

My grandfather said that it was well known that the Chinese were always the greatest and wisest among men. They had invented and discovered everything that was good. Therefore the things which the foreign devils had and the Chinese had not must be evil. Some of these things were very wonderful, enabling the red haired savages to talk with one another, tho they might be thousands of miles apart. They had suns that made darkness like day, their ships carried earthquakes and volcanoes to fight for them, and thousands of demons that lived in iron and steel houses spun their cotton and silk, pushed their boats, pulled their cars, printed their newspapers and did other work for them. They were constantly showing disrespect for their ancestors by getting new things to take the place of the old.

I heard about the American foreign devils, that they were false, having made a treaty by which it was agreed that they could freely come to China, and the Chinese as freely go to their country. After this treaty was made China opened its doors to them and then they broke the treaty that they had asked for by shutting the Chinese out of their country.

When I was ten years of age I worked on my father's farm, digging, hoeing, manuring, gathering and carrying the crop. We had no horses, as nobody under the rank of an official is allowed to have a horse in China, and horses do not work on farms there, which is the reason why the roads there are so bad. The people cannot use roads as they are used here, and so they do not make them.

I worked on my father's farm till I was about sixteen years of age, when a man of our tribe came back from America and took ground as large as four city blocks and made a paradise of it. He put a large stone

wall around and led some streams through and built a palace and
summer house and about twenty other structures, with beautiful *opulent*
bridges over the streams and walks and roads. Trees and flowers, *man .*
singing birds, water fowl and curious animals were within the walls.

The man had gone away from our village a poor boy. Now he
returned with unlimited wealth, which he had obtained in the country
of the American wizards. After many amazing adventures he had
become a merchant in a city called Mott Street, so it was said.

When his palace and grounds were completed he gave a dinner to
all the people who assembled to be his guests. One hundred pigs
roasted whole were served on the tables, with chickens, ducks, geese
and such an abundance of dainties that our villagers even now lick
their fingers when they think of it. He had the best actors from Hong
Kong performing, and every musician for miles around was playing
and singing. At night the blaze of the lanterns could be seen for many
miles.

Having made his wealth among the barbarians this man had
faithfully returned to pour it out among his tribesmen, and he is living
in our village now very happy, and a pillar of strength to the poor.
The wealth of this man filled my mind with the idea that I, too,
would like to go to the country of the wizards and gain some of their
wealth, and after a long time my father consented, and gave me his
blessing, and my mother took leave of me with tears, while my
grandfather laid his hand upon my head and told me to remember and
live up to the admonitions of the Sages, to avoid gambling, bad women
and men of evil minds, and so to govern my conduct that when I died
my ancestors might rejoice to welcome me as a guest on high.

My father gave me $100, and I went to Hong Kong with five other
boys from our place and we got steerage passage on a steamer, paying
$50 each. Everything was new to me. All my life I had been used to
sleeping on a board bed with a wooden pillow, and I found the
steamer's bunk very uncomfortable, because it was so soft. The food
was different from that which I had been used to, and I did not like it at
all. I was afraid of the stews, for the thought of what they might be
made of by the wicked wizards of the ship made me ill. Of the great
power of these people I saw many signs. The engines that moved the
ship were wonderful monsters, strong enough to lift mountains. When

I got to San Francisco, which was before the passage of the Exclusion act, I was half starved, because I was afraid to eat the provisions of the barbarians, but a few days' living in the Chinese quarter made me happy again. A man got me work as a house servant in an American family, and my start was the same as that of almost all the Chinese in this country.

The Chinese laundryman does not learn his trade in China; there are no laundries in China. The women there do the washing in tubs and have no washboards or flat irons. All the Chinese laundrymen here were taught in the first place by American women just as I was taught.

When I went to work for that American family I could not speak a word of English, and I did not know anything about housework. The family consisted of husband, wife and two children. They were very good to me and paid me $3.50 a week, of which I could save $3.

I did not know how to do anything, and I did not understand what the lady said to me, but she showed me how to cook, wash, iron, sweep, dust, make beds, wash dishes, clean windows, paint and brass, polish the knives and forks, etc., by doing the things herself and then overseeing my efforts to imitate her. She would take my hands and show them how to do things. She and her husband and children laughed at me a great deal, but it was all good natured. I was not confined to the house in the way servants are confined here, but when my work was done in the morning I was allowed to go out till lunch time. People in California are more generous than they are here.

In six months I had learned how to do the work of our house quite well, and I was getting $5 a week and board, and putting away about $4.25 a week. I had also learned some English, and by going to a Sunday school I learned more English and something about Jesus, who was a great Sage, and whose precepts are like those of Kong-foo-tsze.

It was twenty years ago when I came to this country, and I worked for two years as a servant, getting at the last $35 a month. I sent money home to comfort my parents, but tho I dressed well and lived well and had pleasure, going quite often to the Chinese theater and to dinner parties in Chinatown, I saved $50 in the first six months, $90 in the second, $120 in the third and $150 in the fourth. So I had $410 at the end of two years, and I was now ready to start in business.

When I first opened a laundry it was in company with a partner, who had been in the business for some years. We went to a town about 500 miles inland, where a railroad was building. We got a board shanty and worked for the men employed by the railroads. Our rent cost us $10 a month and food nearly $5 a week each, for all food was dear and we wanted the best of everything—we lived principally on rice, chickens, ducks and pork, and did our own cooking. The Chinese take naturally to cooking. It cost us about $50 for our furniture and apparatus, and we made close upon $60 a week, which we divided between us. We had to put up with many insults and some frauds, as men would come in and claim parcels that did not belong to them, saying they had lost their tickets, and would fight if they did not get what they asked for. Sometimes we were taken before Magistrates and fined for losing shirts that we had never seen. On the other hand, we were making money, and even after sending home $3 a week I was able to save about $15. When the railroad construction gang moved on we went with them. The men were rough and prejudiced against us, but not more so than in the big Eastern cities. It is only lately in New York that the Chinese have been able to discontinue putting wire screens in front of their windows, and at the present time the street boys are still breaking the windows of Chinese laundries all over the city, while the police seem to think it a joke.

We were three years with the railroad, and then went to the mines, where we made plenty of money in gold dust, but had a hard time, for many of the miners were wild men who carried revolvers and after drinking would come into our place to shoot and steal shirts, for which we had to pay. One of these men hit his head hard against a flat iron and all the miners came and broke up our laundry, chasing us out of town. They were going to hang us. We lost all our property and $365 in money, which members of the mob must have found.

Luckily most of our money was in the hands of Chinese bankers in San Francisco. I drew $500 and went East to Chicago, where I had a laundry for three years, during which I increased my capital to $2,500. After that I was four years in Detroit. I went home to China in 1897, but returned in 1898, and began a laundry business in Buffalo. But Chinese laundry business now is not as good as it was ten years ago.

Laundry
↓
new
business

American cheap labor in the steam laundries has hurt it. So I
determined to become a general merchant, and with this idea I came to
New York and opened a shop in the Chinese quarter, keeping silks,
teas, porcelain, clothes, shoes, hats and Chinese provisions, which
include sharks' fins and nuts, lily bulbs and lily flowers, lychee nuts
and other Chinese dainties, but do not include rats, because it would
be too expensive to import them. The rat which is eaten by the
Chinese is a field animal which lives on rice, grain and sugar cane. Its
flesh is delicious. Many Americans who have tasted shark's fin and
bird's nest soup and tiger lily flowers and bulbs are firm friends of
Chinese cookery. If they could enjoy one of our fine rats they would go
to China to live, so as to get some more.

American people eat ground hogs, which are very like these
Chinese rats, and they also eat many sorts of food that our people
would not touch. Those that have dined with us know that we
understand how to live well.

The ordinary laundry shop is generally divided into three rooms. In
front is the room where the customers are received, behind that a
bedroom and in the back the work shop, which is also the dining room
and kitchen. The stove and cooking utensils are the same as those of
the Americans.

Work in a laundry begins early on Monday morning—about seven
o'clock. There are generally two men, one of whom washes while the
other does the ironing. The man who irons does not start in till
Tuesday, as the clothes are not ready for him to begin till that time. So
he has Sundays and Mondays as holidays. The man who does the
washing finishes up on Friday night, and so he has Saturday and
Sunday. Each works only five days a week, but those are long days—
from seven o'clock in the morning till midnight.

During his holidays the Chinaman gets a good deal of fun out of life.
There's a good deal of gambling and some opium smoking, but not so
much as Americans imagine. Only a few of New York's Chinamen
smoke opium. The habit is very general among rich men and officials
in China, but not so much among poor men. I don't think it does as
much harm as the liquor that the Americans drink. There's nothing so
bad as a drunken man. Opium doesn't make people crazy.

Gambling is mostly fan tan, but there is a good deal of poker, which the Chinese have learned from Americans and can play very well. They also gamble with dominoes and dice.

The fights among the Chinese and the operations of the hatchet men are all due to gambling. Newspapers often say that they are feuds between the six companies, but that is a mistake. The six companies are purely benevolent societies, which look after the Chinaman when he first lands here. They represent the six southern provinces of China, where most of our people are from, and they are like the German, Swedish, English, Irish and Italian societies which assist emigrants. When the Chinese keep clear of gambling and opium they are not blackmailed, and they have no trouble with hatchet men or any others.

About 500 of New York's Chinese are Christians, the others are Buddhists, Taoists, etc., all mixed up. These haven't any Sunday of their own, but keep New Year's Day and the first and fifteenth days of each month, when they go to the temple in Mott Street.

In all New York there are only thirty-four Chinese women, and it is impossible to get a Chinese woman out here unless one goes to China and marries her there, and then he must collect affidavits to prove that she really is his wife. That is in case of a merchant. A laundryman can't bring his wife here under any circumstances, and even the women of the Chinese Ambassador's family had trouble getting in lately.

Is it any wonder, therefore, or any proof of the demoralization of our people if some of the white women in Chinatown are not of good character? What other set of men so isolated and so surrounded by alien and prejudiced people are more moral? Men, wherever they may be, need the society of women, and among the white women of Chinatown are many excellent and faithful wives and mothers.

Recently there has been organized among us the Oriental Club, composed of our most intelligent and influential men. We hope for a great improvement in social conditions by its means, as it will discuss matters that concern us, bring us in closer touch with Americans and speak for us in something like an offical manner.

Some fault is found with us for sticking to our old customs here, especially in the matter of clothes, but the reason is that we find American clothes much inferior, so far as comfort and warmth go. The Chinaman's coat for the winter is very durable, very light and very warm. It is easy and not in the way. If he wants to work he slips out of it in a moment and can put it on again as quickly. Our shoes and hats also are better, we think, for our purposes, than the American clothes. Most of us have tried the American clothes, and they make us feel as if we were in the stocks.

I have found out, during my residence in this country, that much of the Chinese prejudice against Americans is unfounded, and I no longer put faith in the wild tales that were told about them in our village, tho some of the Chinese, who have been here twenty years and who are learned men, still believe that there is no marriage in this country, that the land is infested with demons and that all the people are given over to general wickedness.

I know better. Americans are not all bad, nor are they wicked wizards. Still, they have their faults, and their treatment of us is outrageous.

The reason why so many Chinese go into the laundry business in this country is because it requires little capital and is one of the few opportunities that are open. Men of other nationalities who are jealous of the Chinese, because he is a more faithful worker than one of their people, have raised such a great outcry about Chinese cheap labor that they have shut him out of working on farms or in factories or building railroads or making streets or digging sewers. He cannot practice any trade, and his opportunities to do business are limited to his own countrymen. So he opens a laundry when he quits domestic service.

The treatment of the Chinese in this country is all wrong and mean. It is persisted in merely because China is not a fighting nation. The Americans would not dare to treat Germans, English, Italians or even Japanese as they treat the Chinese, because if they did there would be a war.

There is no reason for the prejudice against the Chinese. The cheap labor cry was always a falsehood. Their labor was never cheap, and is not cheap now. It has always commanded the highest market price. But the trouble is that the Chinese are such excellent and faithful workers that bosses will have no others when they can get them. If you look at men working on the street you will find an overseer for every four or five of them. That watching is not necessary for Chinese. They work as well when left to themselves as they do when some one is looking at them.

It was the jealousy of laboring men of other nationalities—especially the Irish—that raised all the outcry against the Chinese. No one would hire an Irishman, German, Englishman or Italian when he could get a Chinese, because our countrymen are so much more honest, industrious, steady, sober and painstaking. Chinese were persecuted, not for their vices, but for their virtues. There never was any honesty in the pretended fear of leprosy or in the cheap labor scare, and the persecution continues still, because Americans make a mere practice of loving justice. They are all for money making, and they want to be on the strongest side always. They treat you as a friend while you are prosperous, but if you have a misfortune they don't know you. There is nothing substantial in their friendship.

Wu-Ting-Fang talked very plainly to Americans about their ill treatment of our countrymen, but we don't see any good results. We hoped for good from Roosevelt, we thought him a brave and good man, but yet he has continued the exclusion of our countrymen, tho all other nations are allowed to pour in here—Irish, Italians, Jews, Poles, Greeks, Hungarians, etc. It would not have been so if Mr. McKinley had lived.   *treatment*

Irish fill the almshouses and prisons and orphan asylums, Italians are among the most dangerous of men, Jews are unclean and ignorant. Yet they are all let in, while Chinese, who are sober, or duly law abiding, clean, educated and industrious, are shut out. There are few Chinamen in jails and none in the poor houses. There are no Chinese tramps or drunkards. Many Chinese here have become sincere Christians, in spite of the persecution which they have to endure from their heathen countrymen. More than half the Chinese in this country would become citizens if allowed to do so, and would be patriotic Americans. But how can they make this country their home as matters now are! They are not allowed to bring wives here from China, and if they marry American women there is a great outcry.

All Congressmen acknowledge the injustice of the treatment of my people, yet they continue it. They have no backbone.

Under the circumstances, how can I call this my home, and how can any one blame me if I take my money and go back to my village in China?

New York

More Slavery at the South:
A Negro Nurse

A famous character in the folklore of the white South is the black
nursemaid. What follows is a nursemaid's own story, and at virtually
every point it diverges from the stereotype of a dutiful, self-sacrificing
black woman who loved her white family and its children every bit as
much as her own. Economic necessity, not love, compelled her to
work thirty of her forty years for white families. Beginning as a
"house-girl," doing odd jobs and runnng errands, she became, in turn,
a chambermaid, a cook, and, finally, a nursemaid. Like many of the
peons on plantations, she had made a contract with the white family,
only in her case the agreement was oral. It was, however, almost as
binding as a written contract, and it allowed her few opportunities to
be a mother to her own children. "Tho today we are enjoying nominal
freedom," she observed, "we are literally slaves." Working fourteen
to sixteen hours a day and living in with the white family, "I'm on duty
all the time—from sunrise to sunrise, every day in the week." Even
more demoralizing, "I live a treadmill life; and I see my own children
only when they happen to see me on the streets when I am out with the
children, or when my children come to the 'yard' to see me, which isn't
often, because my white folks don't like to see their servants' children
hanging around their premises." She had only a dim prospect for
bettering her life, and there was every possibility that her daughters
would step onto the same treadmill and become lifelong nursemaids.

The nurse received meager wages, and she supplemented her pay
by "taking" for her use a few staples such as sugar, flour, meal, and
soap. She also depended for food on the "service pan," the "left-over"
items from the white family's table, which "is the mainstay in many a
[black] home." Living hand-to-mouth, she could not plan for the
future; it was enough just to try to endure the day-to-day abuses she
suffered as a powerless black woman. A constant indignity, for

Independent, LXXII (Jan. 25, 1912), 196-200.

example, was to be called not by one's name, but rather "nigger" or "Mammy," "Cook," or "Nurse." More disturbing was that "a colored woman's virtue in this part of the country has no protection." White men, unrestrained by law, custom, or by black men armed with the power to retaliate, sexually abused black women. "I believe, " the nurse stated, "[that] all white men take, and expect to take, undue liberties with their colored female servants. . . ." Black women who refused to acquiesce often found themselves jobless; on the other hand, "those who tamely submit to these improper relations live in clover." Concubinage and illegitimacy were widespread in the South, "and the fathers of the new generation of negroes are white men, while their mothers are unmarried colored women."

There was nothing unique about this black nurse's unhappy life. Indeed, she estimated that two-thirds of the blacks in her city of fifty thousand were menial servants, and that two-thirds of the black women there worked for their livelihood, most of them "as nurses, cooks, washerwomen, chambermaids, seamstresses, hucksters, janitresses, and the like." They, too, along with hundreds of thousands of other black women in the South, had to contend with miserly pay, extreme financial dependence on whites, vulnerability to the sexual aggressions of white men, and the torment of neglecting their children while serving those of their white masters and mistresses.[1]

I AM a negro woman, and I was born and reared in the South. I am now past forty years of age and am the mother of three children. My husband died nearly fifteen years ago, after we had been married about five years. For more than thirty years—or since I was ten years old—I have been a servant in one capacity or another in white familes in a thriving Southern city, which has at present a population of more than 50,000. In my early years I was at first what might be called a "house-girl," or, better, a "house-boy." I used to answer the doorbell, sweep the yard, go on errands and do odd jobs. Later on I became a chambermaid and performed the usual duties of such a servant in a home. Still later I was graduated into a cook, in which position I

1. David M. Katzman, *Seven Days a Week: Women and Domestic Service in Industrializing America* (New York, 1978; Urbana, Ill., 1981), 184-222.

served at different times for nearly eight years in all. During the last ten years I have been a nurse. I have worked for only four different families during all these thirty years. But, belonging to the servant class, which is the majority class among my race at the South, and associating only with servants, I have been able to become intimately acquainted not only with the lives of hundreds of household servants, but also with the lives of their employers. I can, therefore, speak with authority on the so-called servant question; and what I say is said out of an experience which covers many years.

To begin with, then, I should say that more than two-thirds of the negroes of the town where I live are menial servants of one kind or another, and besides that more than two-thirds of the negro women here, whether married or single, are compelled to work for a living,— as nurses, cooks, washerwomen, chambermaids, seamstresses, hucksters, janitresses, and the like. I will say, also, that the condition of this vast host of poor colored people is just as bad as, if not worse than, it was during the days of slavery. Tho today we are enjoying nominal freedom, we are literally slaves. And, not to generalize, I will give you a sketch of the work I have to do—and I'm only one of many.

I frequently work from fourteen to sixteen hours a day. I am compelled by my contract, which is oral only, to sleep in the house. I am allowed to go home to my own children, the oldest of whom is a girl of 18 years, only once in two weeks, every other Sunday afternoon— even then I'm not permitted to stay all night. I not only have to nurse a little white child, now eleven months old, but I have to act as playmate or "handy-andy," not to say governess, to three other children in the home, the oldest of whom is only nine years of age. I wash and dress the baby two or three times each day; I give it its meals, mainly from a bottle; I have to put it to bed each night; and, in addition, I have to get up and attend to its every call between midnight and morning. If the baby falls to sleep during the day, as it has been trained to do every day about eleven o'clock, I am not permitted to rest. It's "Mammy, do this," or "Mammy, do that," or "Mammy, do the other," from my mistress, all the time. So it is not strange to see "Mammy" watering the lawn in front with the garden hose, sweeping the sidewalk, mopping the porch and halls, dusting around the house, helping the cook, or darning stockings. Not only so, but I have to put the other

Everywhere in the South white middle-class children were entrusted to the care of black nursemaids. Unfortunately, round-the-clock nurturing of her white charges separated the "Negro Nurse" from her own children. As she explains in "More Slavery at the South," her employer would not allow the nursemaid's children to visit their mother. National Archives.

three children to bed each night as well as the baby, and I have to wash them and dress them each morning. I don't know what it is to go to church; I don't know what it is to go to a lecture or entertainment or anything of the kind. I live a treadmill life; and I see my own children only when they happen to see me on the streets when I am out with the children, or when my children come to the "yard" to see me, which isn't often, because my white folks don't like to see their servants' children hanging around their premises. You might as well say that I'm on duty all the time—from sunrise to sunrise, every day in the week. I am the slave, body and soul, of this family. And what do I get for this work—this lifetime bondage? The pitiful sum of ten dollars a month! And what am I expected to do with these ten dollars? With this money I'm expected to pay my house rent, which is four dollars per month, for a little house of two rooms, just big enough to turn round in; and I'm expected, also, to feed and clothe myself and three children. For two years my oldest child, it is true, has helped a little toward our support by taking in a little washing at home. She does the washing and ironing of two white families, with a total of five persons; one of these families pays her $1.00 per week, and the other 75 cents per week, and my daughter has to furnish her own soap and starch and wood. For six months my youngest child, a girl about thirteen years old, has been nursing, and she receives $1.50 per week but has no night work. When I think of the low rate of wages we poor colored people receive, and when I hear so much said about our unreliability, our untrustworthiness, and even our vices, I recall the story of the private soldier in a certain army who, once upon a time, being upbraided by the commanding officer because the heels of his shoes were not polished, is said to have replied: "Captain, do you expect all the virtues for $13 per month?"

Of course, nothing is being done to increase our wages, and the way things are going at present it would seem that nothing could be done to cause an increase of wages. We have no labor unions or organizations of any kind that could demand for us a uniform scale of wages for cooks, washerwomen, nurses, and the like; and, for another thing, if some negroes did here and there refuse to work for seven and eight and ten dollars a month, there would be hundreds of other negroes right on the spot ready to take their places and do the same work, or more, for

unemployed black : vagrant - send to state farm
slaves

idle person to
visible mean or
support

180   *Plain Folk*

the low wages that had been refused. So that, the truth is, we have to work for little or nothing or become vagrants! And that, of course, in this State would mean that we would be arrested, tried, and despatched to the "State Farm," where we would surely have to work for nothing or be beaten with many stripes!

Nor does this low rate of pay tend to make us efficient servants. The most that can be said of us negro household servants in the South—and I speak as one of them—is that we are to the extent of our ability willing and faithful slaves. We do not cook according to scientific principles because we do not know anything about scientific principles. Most of our cooking is done by guesswork or by memory. We cook well when our "hand" is in, as we say, and when anything about the dinner goes wrong, we simply say, "I lost my hand today!" We don't know anything about scientific food for babies, nor anything about what science says must be done for infants at certain periods of their growth or when certain symptoms of disease appear; but somehow we "raise" more of the children than we kill, and, for the most part, they are lusty chaps—all of them. But the point is, we do not go to cooking-schools nor to nurse-training schools and so it cannot be expected that we should make as efficient servants without such training as we should make were such training provided. And yet with our cooking and nursing, such as it is, the white folks seem to be satisfied—perfectly satisfied. I sometimes wonder if this satisfaction is the outgrowth of the knowledge that more highly trained servants would be able to demand better pay!

Perhaps some might say, if the poor pay is the only thing about which we have to complain, then the slavery in which we daily toil and struggle is not so bad after all. But the poor pay isn't all—not by any means! I remember very well the first and last place from which I was dismissed. I lost my place because I refused to let the madam's husband kiss me. He must have been accustomed to undue familiarity with his servants, or else he took it as a matter of course, because without any love-making at all, soon after I was installed as cook, he walked up to me, threw his arms around me, and was in the act of kissing me, when I demanded to know what he meant, and shoved him away. I was young then, and newly married, and didn't know then what has been a burden to my mind and heart ever since: that a colored woman's virtue in this part of the country has no protection. I at once went home, and told my husband about it. When my husband went to the man who had insulted me, the man cursed him, and slapped him, and —had him arrested! The police judge fined my husband $25. I was present at the hearing, and testified on oath to the insult offered me. The white man, of course, denied the charge. The old judge looked up and said: "This court will never take the word of a nigger against the word of a white man." Many and many a time since I have heard similar stories repeated again and again by my friends. I believe nearly all white men take, and expect to take, undue liberties with their colored female servants—not only the fathers, but in many cases the sons also. Those servants who rebel against such familiarity must either leave or expect a mighty hard time, if they stay. By comparison, those who tamely submit to these improper relations live in clover. They always have a little "spending change," wear better clothes, and are able to get off from work at least once a week—and sometimes oftener. This moral debasement is not at all times unknown to the white women in these homes. I know of more than one colored woman who was openly importuned by white women to become the mistresses of their white husbands, on the ground that they, the white wives, were afraid that, if their husbands did not associate with colored women, they would certainly do so with outside white women, and the white wives, for reasons which ought to be perfectly obvious, preferred to have their husbands do wrong with colored women in order to keep their husbands *straight!* And again, I know at least fifty places in my small town where white men are positively raising two families—a white family in the "Big House" in front, and a colored family in a "Little House" in the backyard. In most cases, to be sure, the colored women involved are the cooks or chambermaids or seamstresses, but it cannot be true that their real connection with the white men of the families is unknown to the white women of the families. The results of this concubinage can be seen in all of our colored churches and in all of our colored public schools in the South, for in most of our churches and schools the majority of the young men and women and boys and girls are light-skinned mulattoes. The real, Simon-pure, blue-gum, thick-lip, coal-black negro is passing away—certainly in the cities; and the fathers of the new generation of negroes are white men, while

offspring - ½ white ½ black

their mothers are unmarried colored women.

Another thing—it's a small indignity, it may be, but an indignity just the same. No white person, not even the little chidren just learning to talk, no white person at the South ever thinks of addressing any negro man or woman as *Mr.,* or *Mrs.,* or *Miss.* The women are called, "Cook," or "Nurse," or "Mammy," or "Mary Jane," or "Lou," or "Dilcey," as the case might be, and the men are called "Bob," or "Boy," or "Old Man," or "Uncle Bill," or "Pate." In many cases our white employers refer to us, and in our presence, too, as their "niggers." No matter what they call us—no matter what they teach their children to call us—we must tamely submit, and answer when we are called; we must enter no protest; if we did object, we should be driven out without the least ceremony, and, in applying for work at other places, we should find it very hard to procure another situation. In almost every case, when our intending employers would be looking up our record, the information would be give by telephone or otherwise that we were "impudent," "saucy," "dishonest," and "generally unreliable." In our town we have no such thing as an employment agency or intelligence bureau, and, therefore, when we want work, we have to get out on the street and go from place to place, always with hat in hand, hunting for it.

Another thing. Sometimes I have gone on the street cars or the railroad trains with the white children, and, so long as I was in charge of the children, I could sit anywhere I desired, front or back. If a white man happened to ask some other white man, "What is that nigger doing in here?" and was told, "Oh, she's the nurse of those white children in front of her!" immediately there was the hush of peace. Everything was all right, so long as I was in the white man's part of the street car or in the white man's coach as a servant—a slave—but as soon as I did not present myself as a menial, and the relationship of master and servant was abolished by my not having the white children with me, I would be forthwith assigned to the "nigger" seats or the "colored people's coach." Then, too, any day in my city, and I understand that it is so in every town in the South, you can see some "great big black burly" negro coachman or carriage driver huddled up beside some aristocratic Southern white woman, and nothing is said about it, nothing is done about it, nobody resents the familiar contact.

But let that same colored man take off his brass buttons and his high hat, and put on the plain livery of an average American citizen, and drive one block down any thoroughfare in any town in the South with that same white woman, as her equal or companion or friend, and he'd be shot on the spot!

You hear a good deal nowadays about the "service pan." The "service pan" is the general term applied to "left-over" food, which in many a Southern home is freely placed at the disposal of the cook or, whether so placed or not, it is usually disposed of by the cook. In my town, I know, and I guess in many other towns also, every night when the cook starts for her home she takes with her a pan or a plate of cold victuals. The same thing is true on Sunday afernoons after dinner— and most cooks have nearly every Sunday afternoon off. Well, I'll be frank with you, if it were not for the service pan, I don't know what the majority of our Southern colored families would do. The service pan is the mainstay in many a home. Good cooks in the South receive on an average $8 per month. Porters, butlers, coachmen, janitors, "office boys" and the like receive on an average $16 per month. Few and far between are the colored men in the South who receive $1 or more per day. Some mechanics do; as for example, carpenters, brick masons, wheelwrights, blacksmiths, and the like. The vast majority of negroes in my town are serving in menial capacities in homes, stores and offices. Now taking it for granted, for the sake of illustration, that the husband receives $16 per month and the wife $8. That would be $24 between the two. The chances are that they will have anywhere from five to thirteen children between them. Now, how far will $24 go toward housing and feeding and clothing ten or twelve persons for thirty days? And, I tell you, with all of us poor people the service pan is a great institution; it is a great help to us, as we wag along the weary way of life. And then most of the white folks expect their cooks to avail themselves of these perquisites; they allow it; they expect it. I do not deny that the cooks find opportunity to hide away at times, along with the cold "grub," a little sugar, a little flour, a little meal, or a little piece of soap; but I indignantly deny that we are thieves. We don't steal; we just "take" things—they are a part of the oral contract, exprest or implied. We understand it, and most of the white folks understand it. Others may denounce the service pan, and say that it is used only to support idle negroes, but many a time, when I was a cook, and had the responsibility of rearing my three children upon my lone shoulders, many a time I have had occasion to bless the Lord for the service pan!

I have already told you that my youngest girl was a nurse. With scores of other colored girls who are nurses, she can be seen almost any afternoon, when the weather is fair, rolling the baby carriage or lolling about on some one of the chief boulevards of our town. The very first week that she started out on her work she was insulted by a white man, and many times since has been improperly approached by other white men. It is a favorite practice of young white sports about town—and they are not always young, either—to stop some colored nurse, inquire the name of the "sweet little baby," talk baby talk to the child, fondle it, kiss it, make love to it, etc., etc., and in nine of ten cases every such white man will wind up by making love to the colored nurse and seeking an appointment with her.

I confess that I believe it to be true that many of our colored girls are as eager as the white men are to encourage and maintain these improper relations; but where the girl is not willing, she has only herself to depend upon for protection. If their fathers, brothers or husbands seek to redress their wrongs, under our peculiar conditions, the guiltless negroes will be severely punished, if not killed, and the white blackleg will go scot-free!

Ah, we poor colored women wage earners in the South are fighting a terrible battle, and because of our weakness, our ignorance, our poverty, and our temptations we deserve the sympathies of mankind. Perhaps a million of us are introduced daily to the privacy of a million chambers thruout the South, and hold in our arms a million white children, thousands of whom, as infants, are suckled at our breasts— during my lifetime I myself have served as "wet nurse" to more than a dozen white children. On the one hand, we are assailed by white men, and, on the other hand, we are assailed by black men, who should be our natural protectors; and, whether in the cook kitchen, at the washtub, over the sewing machine, behind the baby carriage, or at the ironing board, we are but little more than pack horses, beasts of burden, slaves! In the distant future, it may be, centuries and centuries hence, a monument of brass or stone will be erected to the Old Black Mammies of the South, but what we need is present help, present

sympathy, better wages, better hours, more protection, and a chance
to breathe for once while alive as free women. If none others will help
us, it would seem that the Southern white women themselves might do
so in their own defense, because we are rearing their children—we
feed them, we bathe them, we teach them to speak the English
language, and in numberless instances we sleep with them—and it is
inevitable that the lives of their children will in some measure be pure
or impure according as they are affected by contact with their colored
nurses.

Georgia

The Race Problem—An Autobiography:
A Southern Colored Woman

"Everything is forgiven in the South," wrote the author of this life story, "but color." The daughter of a former slave who had become a merchant, the wife of a physician, and the mother of three children, this black woman had concerns both parallel to and different from those of the black nurse. To her, education, hard work, self-reliance, and extreme frugality offered the promise of a self-respecting and productive life, even in the South. This was a hope she shared with her father and her husband, both of whom had enrolled in schools operated in the post-bellum South by the American Missionary Association. Her father had built his own house, and she and her husband had purchased a spacious house for themselves and their children as well as additional property for rental income. It was a source of pride to this woman that she had "never lived in a rented house except for one year. . . ." It was essential, too, that the money earners in her family be financially independent of whites. "My mother and her children," she recalled, "never performed any labor outside of my father's and their own homes." And this was a tradition to which she intended to adhere. "There is no sacrifice I would not make," she wrote, "no hardship I would not undergo rather than allow my daughters to go in service where they would be thrown constantly in contact with Southern white men, for they consider the colored girl their special prey."

This woman had not suffered economic deprivaton, but she was especially sensitive to segregation, unequal access to quality education and public accommodations, and racial insults. Indeed, all forms of degradation and humiliation based on race were repugnant to her, and she had had to endure her share of them. A little white girl with whom she played eventually rebuffed her because she was "colored." A streetcar conductor gruffly told her, to the amusement of the white passengers, not only that she had better move out of the white section and to the rear of the car, but also that "that's what I'm here for—to tell niggers their places when they don't know them." The same day a young elevator operator barked at her: "I guess you can't read; but niggers don't ride in this elevator, we're white folks, we are." W. E. B. Du Bois, the black scholar and civil rights activist, had been similarly rejected from a whites-only elevator and ordered to ride the freight elevator, which was "filled with mops and pans and brooms and pails of filthy water." Du Bois tried to explain his hurt to a couple of white men: "You cannot understand that crawling, beaten feeling, that makes one wish to sneak like a dog under the house and out from the sight of men."[1]

This southern black woman shared the dream of Martin Luther King, Jr., who sixty years later proclaimed to the participants of the March on Washington, "I have a dream that my four little children will one day live in a nation where they will not be judged by the color of their skin but by the content of their character." Pessimistic, however, she saw no prospect of her dream being fulfilled. Racism breached even the funeral of a Sunday school teacher at her church, "a self-sacrificing, noble young woman who had been loved by many." "More flowers for that dead nigger?" a fifteen-year-old white girl had said to her. "I never saw such a to-do made over a dead nigger before." She had wanted to kill that white girl. It was with "dread" that she reared her own children, dread that her daughters would fall victim to sexual entrapment, dread that her son, whatever his talents, would have "few opportunities" to display them. More and more, she had to accept unhappily that, even through education, hard work, and self-reliance, she could not distance her life from "the race problem."

MY FATHER was slave in name only, his father and master being the same. He lived on a large plantation and knew many useful things. The blacksmith shop was the place he liked best, and he was allowed to go there and make little tools as a child. He became an expert blacksmith before he was grown. Before the war closed he had married and was the father of one child. When his father wanted him

1. William M. Tuttle, Jr., ed., "W. E. B. Du Bois' Confrontation with White Liberalism during the Progressive Era," *Phylon,* XXXV (Sept. 1974), 245.

to remain on the plantation after the war, he refused because the wages offered were too small. The old man would not even promise an increase later, so my father left in a wagon he had made with his own hands, drawn by a horse he had bought from a passing horse drover with his own money.

He had in his wagon his wife and baby, some blacksmith tools he had made from time to time, bedding, their clothing, some food, and twenty dollars in his pocket. As he drove by the house he got out of the wagon to bid his father good-by. The old man came down the steps and, pointing in the direction of the gate, said: "Joseph, when you get on the outside of that gate—stay." Turning to my mother, he said: "When you get hungry and need clothes for yourself and the baby, as you are sure to do, come to me," and he pitched a bag of silver in her lap, which my father immediately took and placed at his father's feet on the steps and said, "I am going to feed and clothe them and I can do it on a bare rock." My father drove twenty-five miles to the largest town in the State, where he succeeded in renting a small house.

The next day he went out to buy something to eat. On his way home a lady offered him fifty cents for a string of fish for which he had only paid twenty cents. That gave him an idea. Why not buy fish every day and sell them? He had thought to get work at his trade, but here was money to be made and quickly. So from buying a few strings of fish he soon saved enough to buy a wagon load of fish.

My mother was very helpless, never having done anything in her life except needlework. She was unfitted for the hard work, and most of this my father did. He taught my mother to cook, and he would wash and iron himself at night.

Many discouraging things happened to them—often sales were slow and fish would spoil; many would not buy of him because he was colored; another baby was born and died, and my father came very near losing his life for whipping a white man who insulted my mother. He got out of the affair finally, but had to take on a heavy debt, besides giving up all of his hard earned savings.

My father said after the war his ambition was first to educate himself and family, then to own a white house with green blinds, as much like his father's as possible, and to support his family by his own

It is easy to imagine that this southern black woman, looking straight into the camera's eye, stared back at whites in the same way. As she explains in "The Race Problem," this "Southern Colored Woman," proud of her own and her family's accomplishments, would not accept the subservient position most whites ascribed to blacks. Library of Congress.

efforts; never to allow his wife and daughters to be thrown in contact with Southern white men in their homes. He succeeded.

The American Missionary Association had opened schools by this time, and my father went to night school and sent his wife and child to school in the day.

By hard work and strict economy two years after he left his father's plantation he gave two hundred dollars for a large plot of ground on a high hill on the outskirts of the town.

Three years later I was born in my father's own home, in his coveted white house with green blinds—his father's house in miniature. Here my father kept a small store, was burned out once and had other trials, but finally he had a large grocery store and feed store attached.

envird ∶
good thing
others peopl
wish to have
to one

I have never lived in a rented house except for one year since I've been grown. I have never gone to a public school in my life, my parents preferring the teaching of the patient "New England schoolmarm" to the Southern "poor white," who thought it little better than a disgrace to teach colored children—so much of a disgrace that she taught her pupils not to speak to her on the streets. My mother and her children never performed any labor outside of my father's and their own homes.

To-day I have the same feeling my parents had. There is no sacrifice I would not make, no hardship I would not undergo rather than allow my daughters to go in service where they would be thrown constantly in contact with Southern white men, for they consider the colored girl their special prey.

It is commonly said that no girl or woman receives a certain kind of insult unless she invites it. That does not apply to a colored girl and woman in the South. The color of her face alone is sufficient invitation to the Southern white man—these same men who profess horror that a white gentleman can entertain a colored one at his table. Out of sight of their own women they are willing and anxious to entertain colored women in various ways. Few colored girls reach the age of sixteen without receiving advances from them—maybe from a young "up-start," and often from a man old enough to be their father, a white haired veteran of sin. Yes, and men high in position, whose wives and daughters are leaders of society. I have had a clerk in a store hold my hand as I gave him the money for some purchase and utter some vile request; a shoe man to take liberties, a man in a crowd to place his hands on my person, others to follow me to my very door, a school director to assure me a position if I did his bidding.

It is true these particular men never insulted me but once; but there are others. I might write more along this line and worse things—how a white man of high standing will systematically set out to entrap a colored girl—but my identification would be assured in some quarters. My husband was also educated in an American Missionary Association school (God bless the name!), and after graduating took a course in medicine in another school. He has practiced medicine now for over ten years. By most frugal living and strict economy he saved enough to buy for a home a house of four rooms, which has since been increased to eight. Since our marriage we have bought and paid for two other places, which we rent. My husband's collections average one hundred dollars a month. We have an iron-bound rule that we must save at least fifty dollars a month. Some months we lay by more, but never less. We do not find this very hard to do with the rent from our places, and as I do all of my work except the washing and ironing.

We have three children, two old enough for school. I try to be a good and useful neighbor and friend to those who will allow me. I would be contented and happy if I, an American citizen, could say as Axel Jarlson (the Swedish emigrant, whose story appeared in *The Independent* of January 8th, 1903) says, "There are no aristocrats to push him down and say that he is not worthy because his father was poor." There are "aristocrats" to push me and mine down and say we are not worthy because we are colored. The Chinaman, Lee Chew, ends his article in *The Independent* of February 19th, 1903, by saying, "Under the circumstances how can I call this my home, and how can any one blame me if I take my money and go back to my village in China?"

Happy Chinaman! Fortunate Lee Chew! You can go back to your village and enjoy your money. This is my village, my home, yet am I an outcast. See what an outcast! Not long since I visited a Southern city where the "Jim Crow" car law is enforced. I did not know of this law, and on boarding an electric car took the most convenient seat. The conductor yelled, "What do you mean? Niggers don't sit with white folks down here. You must have come from 'way up yonder. I'm not Roosevelt. We don't sit with niggers, much less eat with them."

I was astonished and said, "I am a stranger and did not know of your law." His answer was: "Well, no back talk now; that's what I'm here for—to tell niggers their places when they don't know them."

Every white man, woman and child was in a titter of laughter by this time at what they considered the conductor's wit.

These Southern men and women, who pride themselves on their fine sense of feeling, had no feeling for my embarrassment and unmerited insult, and when I asked the conductor to stop the car that I might get off, one woman said in a loud voice, "These niggers get more impudent every day; she doesn't want to sit where she belongs."

No one of them thought that I was embarrássed, wounded and outraged by the loud, brutal talk of the conductor and the sneering, contemptuous expressions on their own faces. They considered me "impudent" when I only wanted to be alone that I might conquer my emotion. I was nervous and blinded by tears of mortification which will account for my second insult on this same day.

I walked downtown to attend to some business and had to take an elevator in an office building. I stood waiting for the elevator, and when the others, all of whom were white, got in I made a move to go in also, and the boy shut the cage door in my face. I thought the elevator was too crowded and waited; the same thing happened the second time. I would have walked up, but I was going to the fifth story, and my long walk downtown had tired me. The third time the elevator came down the boy pointed to a sign and said, "I guess you can't read; but niggers don't ride in this elevator; we're white folks here, we are. Go to the back and you'll find an elevator for freight and niggers."

The occupants of the elevator also enjoyed themselves at my expense. This second insult in one day seemed more than I could bear. I could transact no business in my frame of mind, so I slowly took the long walk back to the suburbs of the city, where I was stopping.

My feelings were doubly crushed and in my heart, I fear, I rebelled not only against man but God. I have been humiliated and insulted often, but I never get used to it; it is new each time, and stings and hurts more and more.

The very first humiliation I received I remember very distinctly to this day. It was when I was very young. A little girl playmate said to me: "I like to come over to your house to play, we have such good

times, and your ma has such good preserves; but don't you tell my ma I
eat over here. My ma says you all are nice, clean folks and she'd rather
live by you than the white people we moved away from; for you don't
borrow things. I know she would whip me if I ate with you, tho,
because you are colored, you know."

I was very angry and forgot she was my guest, but told her to go
home and bring my ma's sugar home her ma borrowed, and the rice
they were always wanting a cup of.

After she had gone home I threw myself upon the ground and cried,
for I liked the little girl, and until then I did not know that being "colored"
made a difference. I am not sure I knew anything about "colored." I
was very young and I know now I had been shielded from all
unpleasantness.

My mother found me in tears and I asked her why was I colored,
and couldn't little girls eat with me and let their mothers know it.

My mother got the whole story from me, but she couldn't satisfy me
with her explanation—or, rather, lack of explanation. The little girl
came often to play with me after that and we were little friends again,
but we never had any more play dinners. I could not reconcile the fact
that she and her people could borrow and eat our rice in their own
house and not sit at my table and eat my mother's good, sweet
preserves.

The second shock I received was horrible to me at the time. I had
not gotten used to real horrible things then. The history of Christian
men selling helpless men and women's children to far distant States
was unknown to me; a number of men burning another chained to a
post an impossibility, the whipping of a grown woman by a strong man
unthought of. I was only a child, but I remember to this day what a
shock I received. A young colored woman of a lovely disposition and
character had just died. She was a teacher in the Sunday school I
attended—a self-sacrificing, noble young woman who had been loved
by many. Her coffin, room, hall, and even the porch of her house were
filled with flowers sent by her friends. There were lovely designs sent
by the more prosperous and simple bouquets made by untrained,
childish hands. I was on my way with my own last offering of love,
when I was met by quite a number of white boys and girls. A girl of
about fifteen year said to me, "More flowers for that dead nigger? I

never saw such a to-do made over a dead nigger before. Why, there must be thousands of roses alone in that house. I've been standing out here for hours and there has been a continual stream of niggers carrying flowers, and beautiful ones, too, and what makes me madder than anything else, those Yankee teachers carried flowers, too!" I, a litte girl, with my heart full of sadness for the death of my friend, could make no answer to these big, heartless boys and girls, who threw stones after me as I ran from them.

When I reached home I could not talk for emotion. My mother was astonished when I found voice to tell her I was not crying because of the death of Miss W., But because I could not do something, anything, to avenge the insult to her dead body. I remember the strongest feeling I had was one of revenge. I wanted even to kill that particular girl or do something to hurt her. I was unhappy for days. I was told that they were heartless, but that I was even worse, and that Miss W. would be the first to condemn me could she speak.

That one encounter made a deep impression on my childish heart; it has been with me throughout the years. I have known real horrors since, but none left a greater impression on me.

My mother used to tell me if I were a good little girl everybody would love me, and if I always used nice manners it would make others show the same to me.

I believed that literally until I entered school, when the many encounters I had with white boys and girls going to and from school made me seriously doubt that goodness and manners were needed in this world. The white children I knew grew meaner as they grew older—more capable of saying things that cut and wound.

I was often told by white children whose parents rented houses: "You think you are white because your folks own their own home; but you ain't, you're a nigger just the same, and my pa says if he had his rights he would own niggers like you, and your home, too."

A child's feelings are easily wounded, and day after day I carried a sad heart. To-day I carry a sad heart on account of my children. What is to become of them? The Southern whites dislike more and more the educated colored man. They hate the intelligent colored man who is accumulating something. The respectable, intelligent colored people are "carefully unknown"; their good traits and virtues are never mentioned. On the other hand, the ignorant and vicious are carefully known and all of their traits cried aloud.

In the natural order of things our children will be better educated than we; they will have our accumulations and their own. With the added dislike and hatred of the white man, I shudder to think of the outcome.

In this part of the country, where the Golden Rule is obsolete, the commandment, "Love thy neighbor as thyself" is forgotten; anything is possible.

I dread to see my children grow. I know not their fate. Where the white girl has one temptation, mine will have many. Where the white boy has every opportunity and protection, mine will have few opportunities and no protection. It does not matter how good or wise my children may be, they are colored. When I have said that, all is said. Everything is forgiven in the South but color.

Appendix

List of "Life Stories" Published in the *Independent*

Independent, LIV (1902)

"The Confessions of a Boss" (Apr. 10, 1902), 845-48.

"A Miner's Story" (June 12, 1902), 1407-10.

"A Salesgirl's Story" (July 31, 1902), 1818-21.

"The Sorrows and Joys of a College President," by Charles F. Thwing (Aug. 7, 1902), 1890-94.

"The Native Land of Tricks: The Confessions of a Former Railroad Claim Agent" (Sept. 11, 1902), 2173-78.

"The Negro Problem: How It Appears to a Southern Colored Woman" and "How it Appears to a Southern White Woman" (Sept. 18, 1902), 2221-28.

"The Experience of an Office Seeker" (Sept. 18, 1902), 2245-50.

"The Story of a Sweatshop Girl," by Sadie Frowne (Sept. 25, 1902), 2279-82.

"The Autobiography of a Labor Leader," by James H. Williams (Nov. 6, 1902), 2634-38.

"The Confessions of a Young Author" (Nov. 20, 1902), 2748-52.

"The Biography of a Bootblack," by Rocco Corresca (Dec. 4, 1902), 2863-67.

Independent, LV (1903)

"A Swedish Emigrant's Story," by Axel Jarlson (Jan. 8, 1903), 88-93.

"From the Policeman's Point of View," by a New York Patrolman (Jan. 15, 1903), 146-50.

"The Biography of a Chinaman," by Lee Chew (Feb. 19, 1903), 417-23.

"The Confessions of a Confessor," by a Parish Priest (Mar. 5, 1903), 534-38.

"The Making of a Tramp," by Mariner J. Kent (Mar. 19, 1903), 667-70.

"Experiences and Reflections of a Hackman," by "Cute" McG. (Apr. 2, 1903), 771-75.

"The Confessions of a Woman Professor" (Apr. 23, 1903), 954-58.

"The Story of a Young Syrian" (Apr. 30, 1903), 1007-13.

"A Defense of the Political Boss, by Himself" (Apr. 30, 1903), 1013-17.

"Memories of an Early Girlhood" and "Memories of an Early Boyhood" (May 7, 1903), 1071-80.

"One Day in the Life of an Amish Woman" (June 11, 1903), 1393-98.

"The Story of Two Moonshiners" (July 16, 1903), 1680-84.

"An Indian Boy's Story," by Ah-nen-la-de-ni (July 30, 1903), 1780-87.

"Experiences of a Street Car Conductor" (Aug. 13, 1903), 1920-24.

"The Life of a Jack Tar," by C. J. Hicks (Aug. 20, 1903), 1972-79.

"The True Life Story of a Nurse Girl," by Agnes M. (Sept. 24, 1903), 2261-66.

"The Making of an Anarchist," by Voltarine De Cleyre (Sept. 24, 1903), 2276-80.

"Autobiography of a Football Player" (Nov. 12, 1903), 2683-87.

"Shanghaied," by James H. Williams (Dec. 31, 1903), 3102-07.

Independent, LVI (1904)

"My Life in the Penitentiary" (Feb. 4, 1904), 255-60.

"The New Slavery in the South—An Autobiography," by a Georgia Negro Peon (Feb. 25, 1904), 409-14.

"The Race Problem—An Autobiography," by a Southern Colored Woman (Mar. 17, 1904), 586-89.

"Experiences of the Race Problem," by a Southern White Woman (Mar. 17, 1904), 590-94.

"Observations of the Southern Race Feeling," by a Northern Woman (Mar. 17, 1904), 594-99.

"Fifty Years of a Sponge Fisher's Life," by Carlos Barker (Apr., 21, 1904), 884-91.

"The Dressmaker's Life Story," by Amelia Des Moulins (Apr. 28, 1904), 939-46.

"A Negro Student's Summer Vacation," by Clifford L. Miller (June 16, 1904), 1364-69.

"Spike Riley's Revenge," by James H. Williams (June 23, 1904), 1427-32.

Independent, LVII (1904)

"A Northern Negro's Autobiography," by Fannie Barrier Williams (July 14, 1904), 91-96.

"From Lithuania to the Chicago Stockyards—An Autobiography," by Antanas Kaztauskis (Aug. 4, 1904), 241-48.

"The Story of a Cripple Creek Miner," by Ross B. Moudy (Aug. 18, 1904), 380-82.

"A Washerwoman" (Nov. 10, 1904), 1073-76.

Independent, LVIII (1905)

"The Story of a Fall River Mill Girl," by Gertrude Barnum (Feb. 2, 1905), 241-43.

"One Farmer's Wife" (Feb. 9, 1905), 294-99.

"The Life of a Mormon Girl" (Feb. 23, 1905), 423-30.

"From the Crosstrees to the Stokehold," by James H. Williams (Mar. 2, 1905), 486-95.

"Women on the Farm" (Mar. 9, 1905), 549-54.

"Why I have No Family," by a Childless Wife, and "My Large Family," by an American Mother (Mar. 23, 1905), 654-60.

"The Story of an Irish Cook" (Mar. 30, 1905), 715-17.

"A Cap Maker's Story," by Rose Schneiderman (Apr. 27, 1905), 935-38.

"A Woman Minister's Autobiography" (May 18, 1905), 1122-26.

"The Story of a Summer Hotel Waitress" (June 15, 1905), 1337-43.

Independent, LIX (1905)

"The Chicago Strike," by a Teamster (July 6, 1905), 15-20.

"A Theatrical Press Agent's Confession and Apology" (July 27, 1905), 191-96.

"A Collar Starcher's Story" (Aug. 10, 1905), 305-10.

"The Engineer's Side of It," by an Old Timer (Aug. 24, 1905), 443-46.

"The Confessions of a Japanese Servant" (Sept. 21, 1905), 661-68.

"The Emotions of an Anonymous Writer" (Sept. 28, 1905), 727-30.

"Being a Mormon," by a Mormon (Oct. 19, 1905), 908-11.

"The Story of a Handicapped Life" (Nov. 9, 1905), 1104-08.
"The Smart Set in Winter," by One of the Four Hundred (Nov. 16, 1905), 1146-50.
"A College Professor's Wife" (Nov. 30, 1905), 1279-83.
"The Retort of an Average Woman" (Dec. 14, 1905), 1411-12.

Independent, LX (1906)

"Shall the Professor 'Stay Put,'" by Another College Professor's Wife (Jan. 18, 1906), 161-62.
"Life Story of a Pushcart Peddler" (Feb. 1, 1906), 274-79.
"Inside an Old Ladies' Home" (Feb. 8, 1906), 329-31.
"The Story of One Woman's Life" (Feb. 15, 1906), 374-77.
"Confessons of a Dramatic Critic" (Mar. 1, 1906), 492-97.
"Why I Gave Up My Practice," by a Lawyer (June 28, 1906), 1534-38.

Independent, LXI (1906)

"The Experiences of a Chorus Girl" (July 12, 1906), 80-85.
"The Autobiography of a Country Spinster," by Aunt Jane (Sept. 13, 1906), 621-27.
"The Confessions of a Stockbroker" (Dec. 20, 1906), 1465-69.

Independent, LXII (1907)

"Confessions of an Undistinguished Heretic" (Jan. 10, 1907), 67-71.
"What It Means to Be Colored in the Capital of the United States" (Jan. 24, 1907), 181-86.
"The Confessions of a Stock Speculator," by a Wall Street 'Piker' (Mar. 21, 1907), 669-72.
"The Life Story of a Hungarian Peon" (Sept. 5, 1907), 557-64.

Independent, LXV (1908)

"Life in the Kentucky Mountains," by a Mountaineer (July 9, 1908), 72-82.

Independent, LXIX (1910)

"A Butler's Life Story" (July 14, 1910), 77-82.

Independent, LXXII (1912)

"More Slavery at the South," by a Negro Nurse (Jan. 25, 1912), 196-200.

A Note on the Editors

DAVID M. KATZMAN is professor of history at the University of Kansas. He received the Philip Taft Labor History Prize in 1979 for his book *Seven Days A Week: Women and Domestic Service in Industrializing America.* He is also the author of *Before the Ghetto: Black Detroit in the Nineteenth Century* and coauthor of *Three Generations in 20th Century America.* He has received fellowships from the John Simon Guggenheim Foundation, the Ford Foundation, the National Endowment for the Humanities and the Institute of Southern History, Johns Hopkins University.

WILLIAM M. TUTTLE, JR., is professor of history at the University of Kansas. He is the author of the award-winning *Race Riot: Chicago in the Red Summer of 1919* and of *Great Life Observed: W. E. B. Du Bois.* He has also contributed articles to the *Journal of American History, Journal of Negro History, Labor History, Agricultural History, Phylon, American Studies,* and *Technology and Culture,* among other journals. Tuttle has been a Guggenheim Fellow and a Younger Humanist Fellow of the National Endowment for the Humanities, and he has been a Fellow at the Institute of Southern History, Johns Hopkins University, and the Charles Warren Center, Harvard University. Professors Tuttle and Katzman are among the coauthors of *A Nation and a People,* a forthcoming history of the United States.